Paper Stays Put

Paper Stays Put

A Collection of Inuit Writing

Edited by
Robin Gedalof
Drawings by
Alootook Ipellie

Hurtig Publishers/Edmonton

Hurtig Publishers Ltd.
10560 105 Street
Edmonton, Alberta

Canadian Cataloguing in Publication Data

Main entry under title:
Paper stays put

Some of the pieces have been translated from Inuktitut.

ISBN 0-88830-181-2

1. Canadian literature (English)—Inuit authors.*   2. Inuit
literature—Canada—Translations into English.*   3. English
literature—Translations from Inuit.   I. Gedalof, Robin.

PS8235.I65P36   C810'.8'0897   C80-091009-5
PR9194.5.I5P36

Printed and bound in Canada

Order From:
Koala Books of Canada Ltd.
14327 - 95 A Avenue
Edmonton T5N 0B6 Canada

Contents

Introduction

Several years ago, when the Inuit Tapirisat of Canada (the Eskimo brotherhood) was conducting a research project on communications in the North, one Inuk was asked why he favoured the funding of community newspapers over other forms of communication. He answered: "By ear we forget, but paper stays put," summing up in a few words the major reason for the rapid development of Inuit literature in Canada in the last thirty years.

Eskimos in Canada have been reading and writing in their own language for over a hundred years. Writing wasn't part of traditional Inuit culture, but once missionaries had devised various systems for putting Inuktitut on paper, the People took to it with enthusiasm. First they used it for religious study, and then for trading, marking graves, and signing the inevitable government chits. Parents taught their children to read, using sooty fingers on white igloo walls to draw the pot hook syllabics or the roman alphabet. When the children grew a little and travelled out to school, leaving their families for months or years at a time, those precious lessons were often their only link with home. Perhaps once or twice a year, a nurse or a trader or an RCMP officer would seek out the students in their school residences and deliver a slip of paper, folded into a tiny wedge, and collect one to be delivered a thousand miles away months later. Those days are gone now. Few people live on the land any more, and most Arctic communities have well-equipped schools, but the Inuit still retain their language and have won the battle to have Inuktitut taught as an integral part of their children's education.

In the meantime, several generations of Inuit writers have worked to preserve their culture, express their views, and communicate with their neighbours in the North and South. At first, short poems or articles by Inuit were published in educational magazines, more as curiosities than anything else. As an English consultant for the Quebec Protestant School Board once half-jokingly put it, natives who could write "anything better than their name" had literary opportunities. But Inuit writers weren't content to be just novelties. They began to publish their work in their own community newsletters and papers. People like Mary Panegoosho, who founded *Inuktitut* magazine, began to seriously promote written material by Inuit, for Inuit, in the Inuit language. The government eventually responded with support for these projects, but the impetus came from the people in the settlements. Readers in the South first became aware of the development of Canadian Inuit literature when the Eskimo pilot Markoosie published his first novel, *Harpoon of the Hunter*, in English in 1970. *Harpoon of the Hunter* is now available in a dozen languages, but it was first serialized in the author's own language in *Inuktitut* magazine. A dozen books and many hundreds of stories, articles, and poems by Inuit writers have appeared since then, and Inuit literature is well on its way to becoming a vital, exciting part of the Canadian cultural mosaic.

Inuit writing today is basically a literature of cross-cultural contact. It is virtually impossible for an Eskimo to write of his life, his problems, his triumphs or his interests, without being aware of his unique position as a time traveller, a product of a stone-age culture in an atomic-age world. The very earliest Inuit writing was simply oral literature recorded on paper, but before long Inuit storytellers and poets began to see the endless possibilities inherent in a written language. Increasingly, their work displayed growing technical control and an extraordinary understanding of the writer's craft. They began to record their impressions of the Southern culture that was having such an impact on their traditional lifestyle, and as contact and settlement increased they began to document their own culture to prevent it being lost. As Inuit became aware of their unique historical position, they began to write about their own personal experiences, realizing that only in each person's individual response could the response of a people be captured.

The movement from recording a traditional chant *verbatim* to writing a complex novel or play in English is not a simple literary process. While many Inuit were helping to build radar stations and airfields in the Arctic, many others were still travelling to their hunting grounds by dog team. People in the west had established hunting and trading agreements with the crews of whaling vessels hundreds of years before, while many Inuit of the central Arctic had never seen a white man. Similarly, while some writers were typing up their autobiographies, other Inuit were just discovering how to read the Bible and to print out their names in syllabics. The range of Inuit experience is captured in the diversity of Inuit literature.

This anthology tries to mirror that complexity. The great variety of material here is a reflection of the subjects and styles adopted by Inuit writers, and while this book is intended to present some of the best of what is available in Inuit writing today, the material could also be said to be typical. It was a temptation to divide the book up into generic or thematic sections, but that would have been to impose a structure that doesn't exist in fact.

The material presented here was chosen not solely because of the merit of the individual pieces, but also because of the way that they worked together. Poetry is balanced against prose, fiction against non-fiction, youth against age, and so on. It is hoped that readers will be able to open the anthology at any point and be drawn both forward and backward. If readers are able to dip into the book at random and come up with unexpected and delightful surprises, then they will be recreating the experience many Northern enthusiasts have had upon first discovering Inuit literature.

This is a book by Eskimos. Some of the material was written in English, some was written in Inuktitut, almost all of it has been published bilingually. But regardless of which language it originated in, it doesn't read like English Canadian literature. Inuit don't speak English like people in the South, and they don't write like people in the South, but Eskimo English has a particularly rich flavour that deserves attention and regard. Consequently, most of the material present in this volume has been allowed to retain its "errors". Translations are sometimes rough, the grammar is occasionally execrable, but it was felt that it would have been a disservice to both the authors and their audience to tidy things up.

There are short introductory notes to each piece which are intended to give some idea of the context in which these songs, stories and essays exist. It is hoped that readers will be encouraged to look for more material by these writers in other publications. A short list of recommended works by Inuit authors has been included in this book, as well as some suggestions for reading on the subjects of Inuit literature and society in general.

This anthology is the result of a co-operative effort, and particular thanks are due to John MacDonald and the staff of the Cultural and Linguistics Section of the Department of Indian and Northern Affairs in Ottawa, and Mick Mallon and the staff of the

Linguistic Development Program of the Department of Education, Government of the Northwest Territories. Alootook Ipellie's major contribution is evident everywhere in the book, and it is my sincere hope that he, and the other authors whose work is represented here, will be as pleased to see these pieces in print again as I am.

ROBIN GEDALOF

Where Are the Stories of My People?
Mary Panegoosho

*As a child, Mary Panegoosho lived with her uncle, Joe Panipakut-
tuk, whose "The Many Lives of Anakajuttuq" appears later in this
volume and who instilled in her a deep appreciation of Inuit
folklore. Her love of the old legends found an outlet when she
became editor of the Eskimo language magazine* Inuktitut. *Her
writings have appeared in many publications. This essay comes
from* North, *September 1962.*

Someone who cared about their language asked one of these
hunters, "What will you do when you get out of hospital?" "Oh,
you must know that I sit waiting for the moon to turn back for me
so that I can go to my home and listen again to the stories of my
people. Oh that I could sit again listening to the stories which come
from a great distance. For this is the time for telling stories. First I
must sit cooling my arms so that the tiredness can go out of me, and
then I must listen, waiting for the story to come, for the story I
want to hear. The mountains may be between us but I will turn
around on my feet. I will turn back on my tracks and, listening,
open my ears to feel the story that comes in on the wind. Oh that I
may listen again to the story that is the wind." Now this comes
straight out of the Stone Age heart. He was homesick above all, not
for his people, not for his country even, but for the stories of his
people.

Akeeko Is Writing
Akeeko

This piece, from Northern Welfare 62; A Symposium on Northern Social Work, *was written by Akeeko in 1962 to try to help Southern welfare officials understand the problems his people face in the North. He describes the traditional, co-operative way of living in the North and how it has been disrupted by Southern settlers.*

At the time I was born, and when I first began to understand, there were no white people in my land. At times white people would visit in boats from Scotland and America, and at times their boats would get stuck in the ice for the whole winter. In those days no one spoke English and there were no schools. The only English words I knew were the names of the visiting white men; names like Billy. I don't know where they went when they left us. I was not hungry in those days because my father was a very good hunter. I was well dressed. My father used to tell me that there was hunger in the days before I was born because there were no guns. My father had a gun but not many cartridges when I was born. Sometimes the boat would bring cartridges, but they would not last all winter.

As I remember, my father would go along in the white men's boats. One time, they didn't return for a whole year because of ice. Where we were staying there was a lot of game. There was polar bear, caribou, wolf, fox—any kind of animal. While my father was away, I stayed with my uncle, mother and one of my oldest sisters. It was during the same winter that we were getting impatient, or rather feared that the boat would never come back. We were running out of food. I myself didn't know how to hunt.

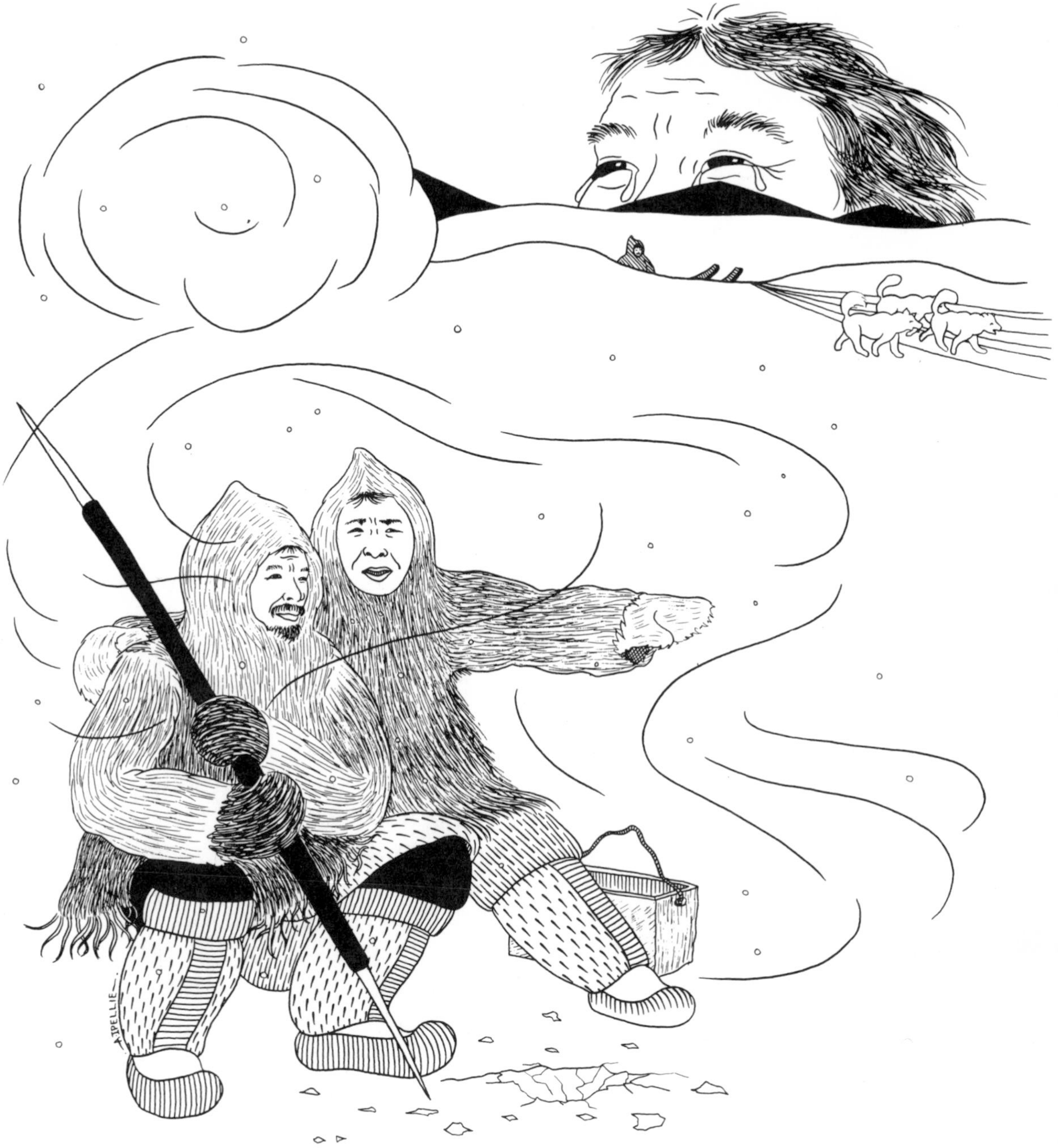
A. IPELLIE

During that winter, mother, sister and I decided to go to the Post. The weather was bad and there were blizzards. Our food would not last us and then I did not know how to kill fox. There I would sit on the icy floor, mother trying to feed me. I sat there all day long. My sister would be crying all day long because my mother did not have milk in her breast. You cannot tell whether a child knows emptiness, but it does and that is why my sister cried most of the time not knowing, or sort of knowing.

In August, the ice broke up. There were lots of seals then and we were not hungry. My father arrived by dog team during a storm. He had found our deserted camp. At the time, we were cutting a hole in the ice to get salt water to cook seal meat. My father followed our sled tracks, accompanied by two other men. He was the leader of the team. I saw my father's head first and I knew him right away. I could not believe he was alive. When I realized, looking at him real and alive, I just started to cry.

In August, we went back to camp because the game was there. But there were no white people. I learned how to hunt and we had no shortage of food. There was no white men's food, except a little flour, tea and matches. To buy these things, we had to trade bear skin and fox. We made clothing out of caribou skin. Although I learned to hunt, I still had to listen to my father's commands and learn many things. When the white people returned, they brought more Eskimos from other places and at the same time, I got my own dogs. By then, my father had a boat too.

Now there were whites and Eskimos, and the caribou were fading away. And I, understanding more, tried to get more and more foxes because there was a Hudson's Bay store now. I tried to get lots knowing that a little will only trade a little. We could now buy material for clothes. To us the material was useful and most precious and we took care of it because there was nothing else we

16 *Akeeko*

could use. Four years later, the caribou were scarce. Even with a dog team we were unable to find any. They were dying by themselves. The Eskimos were saying that they had too much salt water. But I did not believe this.

I didn't have the knowledge of the white men. But I learned to run their boat. I did not know how to repair mechanical things. There was still no caribou when I decided to go to Chesterfield to get myself a wife. Father and mother, and another couple came along. When we got there, most of the Eskimos were ill. It was hard to leave them.

My wife and I were happy and well. We were married July 1, 1931. The caribou were scarce but somehow I did not miss them. Next summer, my wife and I had a little girl. I got six caribou then. We also had lots of walrus meat, seals and flour. During that summer, my father got sick. All the Eskimos were having sore throats. We were living in huts made out of earth. Everything seemed to come at once—no proper home, people sick, no money. We tried to get debt but we could not get it. There was no money for food and nothing to trade.

Many Eskimos died that winter. My mother died too. My father was infected on his face and I had to cut his face to get the discharge out. One of the men at the Post gave me medicine which brought my father's temperature down. It helped him and he was well again. But my mother was dead.

My relatives were staying at the Post and I went and stayed with other Eskimos. As it was winter, it was hard on my strength and there were no foxes. Still, the other Eskimos seemed worse off than I was.

Summer came again. My father lived with us and was not very well. He got two infections on his back. I did what I had done last time but could not help him. At the same time, my wife got blind.

Father could not sleep and he asked that I stay up by his side. I got very tired not getting enough sleep. I fell asleep on the floor and my father died while I slept. My efforts to help him did not work.

It was much harder now and still no foxes. During spring, we moved to the Post but were no better off. I had a gun but no cartridges. I used seal nets and was able to kill a few whales. It was summer then and all the Eskimos were waiting for the boat to come. I myself anxiously waited for the boat because I had a few whale skins to trade. But I also had to give away some of the skins to other Eskimos so they could get tea, flour and sugar.

Winter arrived again and we had to move to where we usually went during the winter. Our dogs were hungry and although I had a boat and motor, I could not use them. I believed there were no caribou but, as I was travelling, I saw caribou tracks. I got caribou and later, polar bear. While hunting, I would sometimes stay away more than a day. I used rags stuffed with earth for a blanket. But I was not sick or hungry like I was when my father died.

After the death of my father and mother, I had four children. The same year, I became sick almost to death. While I was sick, I got $5.00 from the white men. But this was not enough and I went to work for the soldiers. For two years I did not feel well, I was spitting blood and knew I had bad lungs. In April of 1950, I went out to the hospital. For three years, I was a bed patient and in 1954, I had an operation. Part of my lungs were taken out. Later, I got a lung infection and needed another operation. I had a big scar and inside me I was sore. My voice got very low.

I often remember the days long ago when things were different. We were much healthier then. At times it was hard but we were happy. It is so much harder now. But thank you very much for the help I'm getting from the teachers. My grandchildren will live through it, if they don't get sick.

This is Akeeko writing. Other Eskimos know much more than

I do but they do not write. But I know their way of life. Some work now but what they earn goes away fast. I know because lots of them come and tell me. And now they want stoves for the winter. I tell them to ask the teachers but many won't. I cannot help them though I feel sorry for them—especially the ones who are in need.

Our country is now full of white people. The storekeeper cannot trade things cheap now. Now the teacher scolds our children. Mothers and fathers do not approve of this. But perhaps this is necessary. They are doing what they think is best. But this is not approved by Eskimos. We don't know or understand the ways of white men. When bad things happen, we think of telling the Police or the Government. They come once a year and sometimes are told. But are we believed? We are told that we complain about things that are not important. We are told that the young Eskimos will have a much better life when they grow up and will know better than their elders. When somebody finds that this is not true, there will be anger.

Last summer, Eskimos were asked about moving to the DEW Line. Some did not want to go and some wanted to. I know what help they really need. They need money. Possibly some could get money by trapping foxes. But foxes are not plentiful. One has to go very far to get a fox. To do this, it is necessary to leave a wife and children behind without fuel to burn. It is not like it was long ago. Some Eskimos hunt well and some don't. I know myself now how hard it is to do what I used to do. It is also hard not understanding and yet sort of knowing the meaning in English. I have never been to school. Some Eskimos work very hard and some don't. Some have sense and some don't. Others help each other. This is the way it is in our country.

Since I have been to hospital, quite a few Eskimos have gone and have come back. But they are cold and weak when they return. It won't be even a year before they have to return to hospital again.

Akeeko 19

They become sick by trying to hunt foxes to get money to live. They spit blood all over again. Being in hospital once myself, I try to tell them not to work too hard so they won't have to go back to hospital. One of them is my son.

In our country, no one had difficulty in walking. Now people return with weak legs. Their arms are not weak because they are asked to carve in the hospitals. I am sure people could make money out of carving and have warm houses. It is hard for them to come back and be cold. Some of us can get wood to burn but not those who have been in hospital. Wood does not last long. It is harder to get wood since the white men came because they destroyed wood. And there are more Eskimos than there were before.

If Eskimos had boats, they could at least go to salt water and hunt. If we had nets, we could get fish. There are fish in Southampton. This would be a big help. Now that the white man has changed our life, we need help. The white men are building some houses. The house goes to Eskimos the white man thinks are sensible. But some Eskimos will be demanding more and more. Some Eskimos will not think about work but they will demand.

I could very well profit by the ways of the white men but I am an Eskimo. The white men here are more concerned with their work. It would be so much better if they talked to us about things. The written explanations we get are hard to follow. That is why the things we are asked to do are never done. It would be better if we were told by tongue. Eskimos do not pay attention to written things—not even myself.

Older Eskimos used to teach young men how to hunt and how to divide food and how to judge the weather. The older women taught the young ones to sew. Nobody does that now and there are more Eskimos than there were before. There are no caribou and we need skins for clothing. There are no more foxes. The Eskimos need help.

The Little Arctic Tern, the Big Polar Bear
Leah Idlout

Leah Idlout d'Argencourt has been an editor with the magazine Inuit Today *since 1975. When she was twelve years old, she came South from Baffin Island to receive medical treatment. After a year in hospital she returned to her father's camp, but she never forgot the difficulty she had reconciling the cultures of the North and the South. This story was first published in 1959. The translation is by Minnie Aodla Freeman, author of* Life Among the Qallunaat.

It was during spring time when a big polar bear was looking for food. She had been walking for a long way and yet had not found anything. As she was walking on land she felt very tired and warm. It was a very fine day, she decided to rest on the ground. When she felt rested, she started to walk again, wondering where to go. She could see miles away and it was very nice land, the kind of land anybody would want to go to. She had been walking for a long time and still did not know where to go. Then she saw something white. She knew it was not snow as there was none. She knew it was some kind of animal and decided to go to it very silently. The big polar bear was now very careful as she was very hungry, she could only think of eating it, but as she got near she realized it was a little Arctic tern. Why does she not fly away, and not even look afraid even though she just woke up when the bear reached her? The big polar bear wanted so much to eat her.

The big polar bear asked: "Why, on such a nice day, are you just sleeping?"

The tern answered, "I am nesting my egg. I was with my friends when we were going where we usually lay eggs. I didn't get there in time and so I had my egg alone and didn't want to leave as I love it and that's how I happen to be alone here."

The bear asked, "Why do you animals that can fly never leave your eggs alone?"

The tern replied, "Because we dearly love what is alive in our eggs. Also because people go all over the place looking for eggs to eat, we nest our eggs every spring but we don't want them to be taken away. We want them to hatch quickly and because animals also look for eggs."

The polar bear felt very sorry for the tern who was alone like her and where there was nothing and could not even go anywhere.

The tern asked the bear, "Would you mind my egg while I go rest without worry? I will be right back as soon as I find food."

The bear told the tern, "I cannot nest as I am too heavy and I am afraid I will break it. But I can mind it, for everybody is afraid of me—all animals are, even people."

The tern said, "My flying won't take me long to go far in short time. I'll look for seals for us to eat. When I find any I will come back and tell you where and you can go and get them."

They both were very happy over their being able to help each other and so when the little tern had gone the big polar bear felt very sorry for the one little helpless egg. It is well known other birds have usually more than one egg, but the little tern has only one.

The big bear thought to herself, "I have long fur. Even though I am heavy I won't break the egg if I just use my fur to nest it and it will be just as warm."

Night had come and the little tern had not arrived. She had forgotten her egg; all this time she had been with her bird mates and was feeling very happy not being alone. It made her forget about her egg. A month had passed and she had not returned.

22   *Leah Idlout*

And then the bear was seen by hunters. They had come to her very silently as it was a very nice day. She did not move, even though she was wide awake.

The hunters were bothering her, but as she didn't even scare them they asked her, "What are you doing?"

"I am nesting."

The hunter and his son started to laugh, "The bear is nesting."

And the bear began to cry because she was sorry for the egg. Well! when the bear began to cry the man and his son stopped laughing and left as they were too astounded. They are good hunters but all their lives they never saw a bear who can talk, nest an egg, and even cry; they didn't want to kill her. The hunter and his son turned homewards and started off. On the rear of the sled a seal was tied to it; the bear bit it and managed to pull it off and ate it. The hunters didn't even notice—they were still too astonished. They told all the other Eskimos about the bear and they didn't have anything more to do with them. They were afraid.

Two months passed and the egg's mother had not returned. And so the time had come for the birds to go and the bear was still nesting and she didn't even know when it was going to hatch as she never had an egg before. She nested it all winter and following spring. She was very hungry and very thin. She decided to go look for seal and as she started to get up she heard something crack! Of course it was the egg who was hatching. At the same time it was yawning. The big bear only thought it broke; its mother had not arrived and she had said that she never left her eggs alone. The bear was staring at the little new bird. When it appeared she was expecting to see a full bird but it had a bear's head and it was shaking off the broken shells and it had wings and body like bear. It was no wonder—the bear had nested the egg all year and it had turned into a bear. The bear felt very happy as she never had children, and this was her first one. It had wings but that did not

Leah Idlout 23

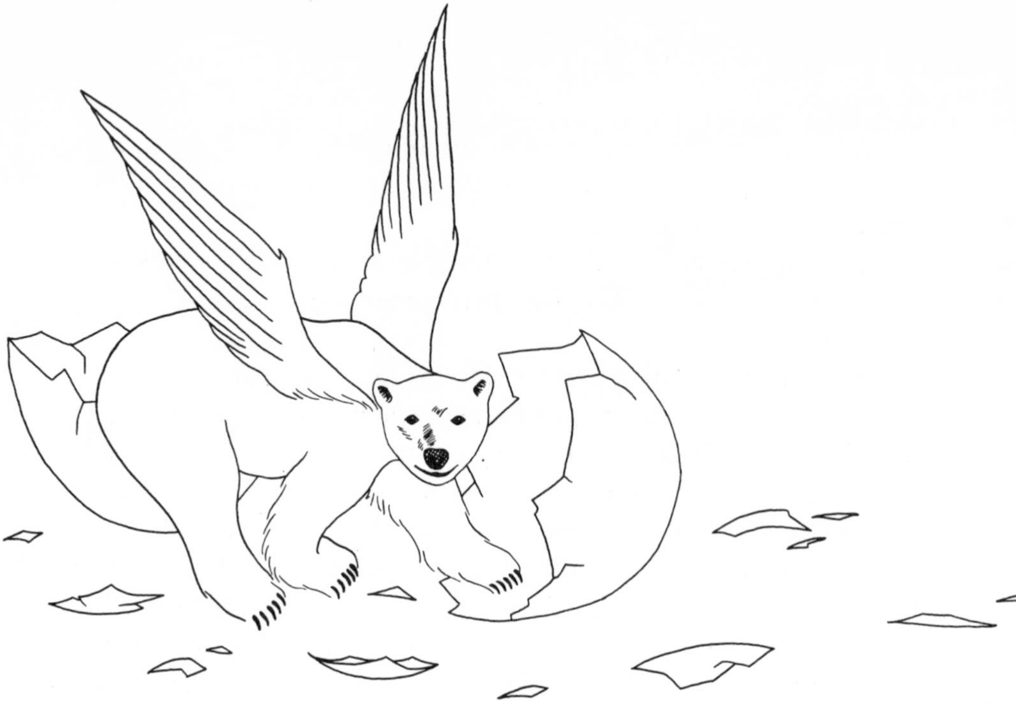

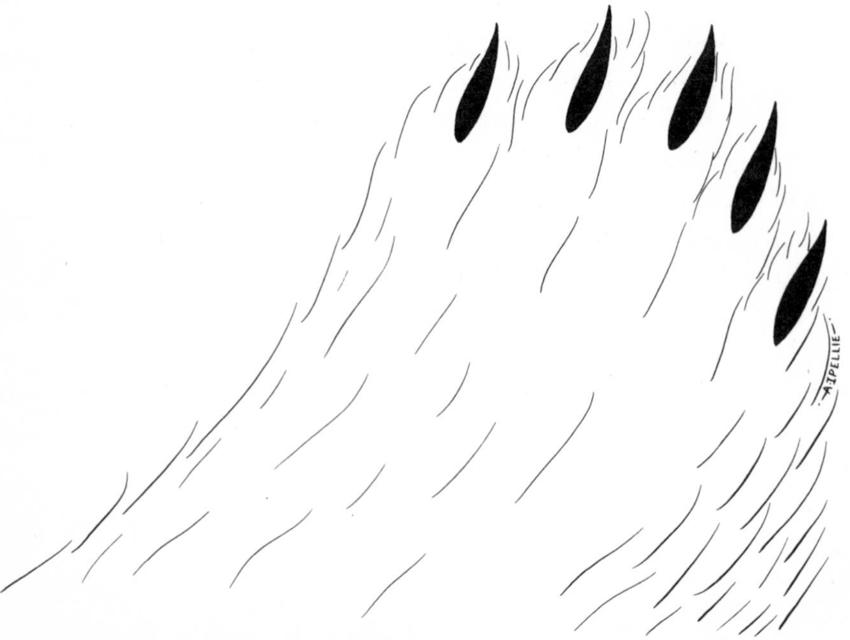
A.IPELLIE

shame her, she just felt like loving it. And then they planned to look for food.

What-was-an-egg-before was able to fly even though he looked like a bear, but he was not mean. The big bear, who was his mother now, now loved all birds because her child was a bird, but looked like a bear. But bears and birds were afraid of the bear-bird. And they didn't want to play with him, so his mother and he were always together.

Whenever he hunted for food he would fly. They ate seals and did not kill birds, but even though he did not kill birds they were afraid of him as there was no such a thing as a bear with wings, yet they wanted to be friendly.

It was time again for his bird mother to go away for the winter. The bear-bird wanted to go too but the big bear did not want to. She had lived all her life in Eskimo land. Her child had some idea he belonged among the birds and wanted to go where they go for winter. The big bear felt very unhappy. She loved him so much, like he was her own. And her child only thought he was just a bird as he had wings. He cannot see himself because they had no mirror. He does not even know he's partly bear.

He was now very big, so he told the big bear he could carry her on his back. He has wings and he can go very far. He wanted to leave before winter came.

And so the big bear went because she did not want to be left behind and because she still felt he was a child even though he had grown.

They arrived at the white man's land. There were so many people and they didn't know where the birds go, and even would lose their way if they go back to Eskimo land. They were on white man's land away beyond Canada. His former mother had such long way to go for winters!

Leah Idlout 25

And then they were seen by white people. People were amazed to see Eskimo bear in white man's land and were fascinated with the one with wings. They were put in a circus so white people can see them. The big bear was confused, she had never seen so many things and never seen so many people in all her life. Her child felt very happy as he had playmates. And so they travelled from one place to another.

It was during winter when they arrived where the little mother tern usually went. The former egg did not know his little mother tern's land. He had never been there, and the big bear did not know either. It was just then the little mother tern was looking for place to sleep. She noticed a circus and went to it. The tern recognized the big bear and went to it. The tern recognized the big bear on account of her child who had wings like her. She remembered the bear was to mind her egg. She was so sorry! Her former egg was actually a little bit a bear. She wanted him back very bad because he had wings and yet she was happy because the big bear minded it very well. But they had big argument. The big bear did not want to let him go. She loved him so much now. And what-was-an-egg-before did not know if the little tern was his mother or not, he didn't even know her, and so his real mother went away.

And now, time to go again to another place, in white man's land. They were both taken and put in their house. But the little mother tern was not taken. They were travelling again and both very happy. They were both well taken care of and both were singing away:

Again, again, it's going to snow,
Again, again, it's going to snow,
How do we know it's going to snow?
Because it always snowed before.

Song of Markoosie
Markoosie

This song was written by the old hunter Markoosie almost forty years ago. He had just lost his eyesight and was in hospital at Chesterfield Inlet. It was first printed in his own language in Inuktitut in 1967.

The north wind is blowing, the night is very cold—ayaiya ya ya
I hear the people passing outside the entrance stairs.
When I come in I go up to the big house, main floor,
When I go out all I do is go as far as the entrance way.
How I wish I could join the hunters, instead of being here
Early to bed is far from fun, here at the Sister's place
All too often I wonder how I could ever see again
There is no song in me, I know, while all around me others sing.

A Spring Seal Hunt
Eepilk

Eepilk was born in 1923 on the southern shore of Admiralty Inlet, and now makes his headquarters at Arctic Bay. Like Peter Pitseolak and others, he keeps a syllabic diary and these extracts reflect the hunting life he leads. They were first published in North *magazine in 1969.*

March 12, 1965
It was a beautiful cloudless day. I missed one seal twice and that was the end of my patience for this day. The first time I was just getting ready to aim, when it came up and of course it saw me right away. I left and came back when it was about time for it to come up, but I just missed it. I fixed up the snow and left because I was getting cold. By chance it will come up again but I won't be there. Tonight I made a rabbit fur sole covered with a flour bag to put under my feet when I wait for that seal again.

March 13
This morning there was a freezing fog. I thought to myself, I don't think I will catch that seal in this weather. The freezing fog makes the snow crisp and the seal will hear Akiti and me. If we don't catch any seals soon we will have to go to our cache and get some whale meat. We decided to go and look for other seal holes and we found several good ones. They ranged quite far but we know where they are now.

March 14
Today is a nice clear day. It is Sunday so we gathered in my house,

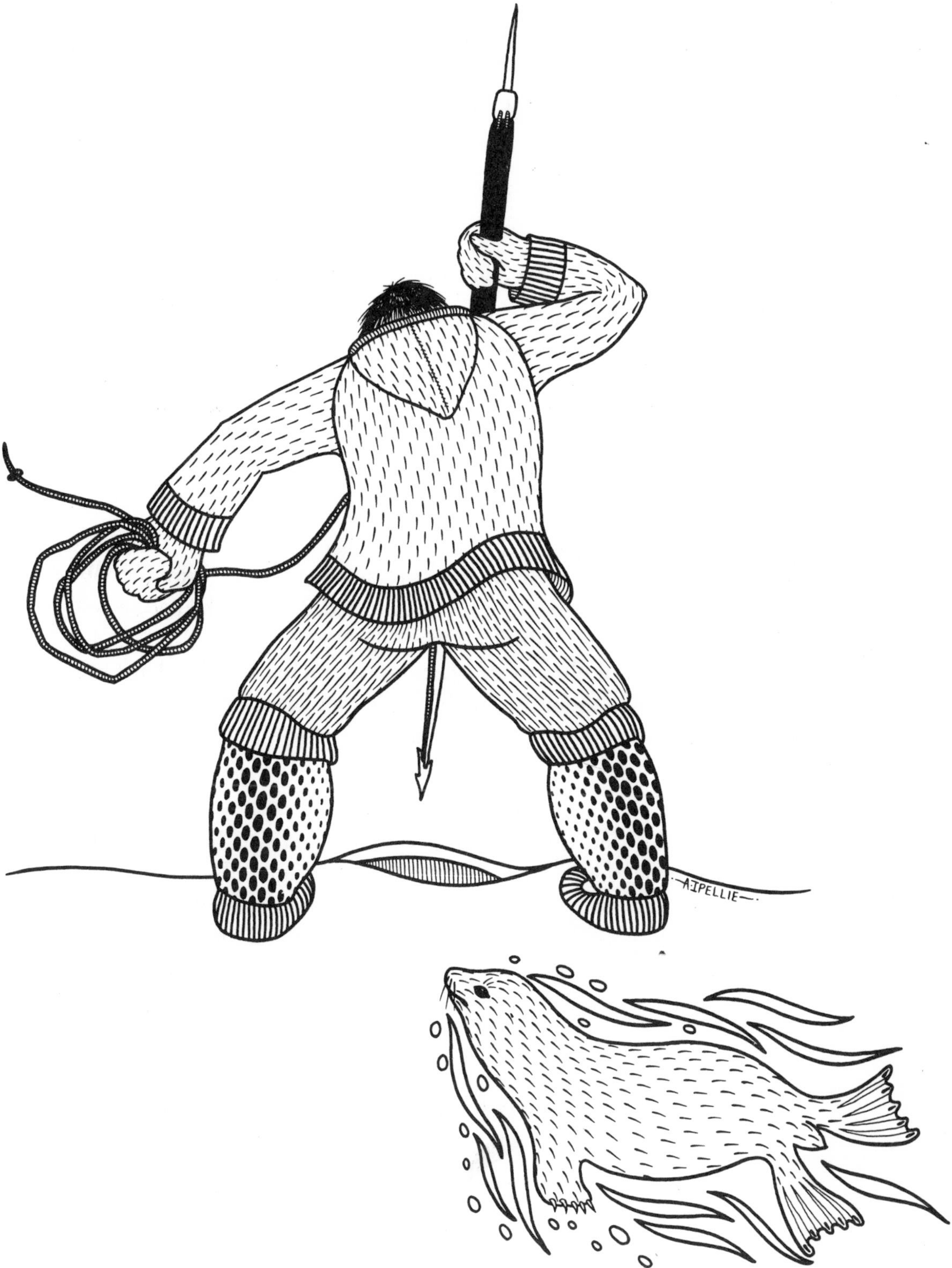
A.IPELLIE

said our prayers that night and discussed our plans. Akiti and I will go to the Hudson's Bay post; in the meantime the rest of the camp will hunt seals.

March 15

This morning the wind was blowing from our back so it was not too cold on our way to the post. Akiti was ahead of me for a long while but that night I went ahead and stayed in front of him until we got to Ikpiajuk the next morning. It took us sixteen hours and everybody was still asleep. We did not even have to tie up the dogs so we just unharnessed them, took the two hundred and thirty-five fox pelts we had and went inside our friend's house.

March 16

Today Akiti and I went to the store and bought our supplies. We went visiting around while our dogs rested. Most of the people had colds as usual. We found out that Ulajuk was going to look at his traps and Kanukulu, my brother-in-law and my sister had just left. We had passed them that night while they were camping. Ulajuk will come with me since Akiti had some work.

March 17

Ulajuk and I left this morning. Ulajuk's sled was heavily loaded and one side of it dragged. We camped near Igalulik. That night it got very dark and windy, the new moon did not help much. The north wind was blowing hard so we just stopped for some tea and kept on going to our settlement. We reached our settlement before everybody was asleep.

March 18

We did not go anywhere today just fixed up our equipment and gave our dogs a rest. The dogs ate two large seals. My ropes had been cut from the rough ice so I was busy all day fixing them. Although the sky was clear there was an icy breeze and a snow drift which was not good for seal hunting. This weather makes me long for the spring so that we can move to our hunting quarters. The drifting snow got worse until it became a blizzard that night.

March 20
Kunuk and his companions came in today. Our sled tracks saved them from getting lost in this blizzard. We placed them at Ulajuk's house. Innijuk had had to kill most of his dogs. His one-year-old dog had gone mad and although it left the camp to die, the sickness had spread to the other dogs.
Soon we will be able to go to the floe-edge. Innijuk will join me with the remainder of his dogs and since his sled is only about four yards long that would be better for him.

March 23
We went to Tikiragjuk today. I had caught eight foxes on the trap line. In the afternoon I shot a real seal on the ice. When the dogs heard my shot, they came running with the sleds and all. My companions left their holes too, to join me. We had some tea and packed our sleds. I fixed up the seal hole so other seals will use it again. As the sun had gone down we headed home soon after. It got dark and hazy. At home the people were playing tag. This raised our spirits up.

March 24
This time when we went to Annuna, the cracked ice had frozen over. We get three seals there: my brother-in-law, Mingijuk and me. I got one with the rifle that had been fixed. It's so amazing when those old fixed rifles can shoot a seal. It is a tricky business,

just like netting fish in the winter. In 1961 when I was fixing a rifle it went off on its own. Oh, that was a near miss. I had not been taught to fix a rifle and when it went off it scared the hell out of me. I would not advise anybody to try it unless they had been taught by someone else.

March 25
As usual I went out this morning when I got up. The blizzard was blowing right from the front. That lowered my spirits to go anywhere. This kind of weather always makes me feel out of sorts. The blowing snow was seeping in through the openings in the door and dogs crowded in the front. We made a porch that helped but it was still cold. That night the gusts of wind calmed down to one main stream although the clouds were moving fast.

April 3
We have found many tracks for the last two days. Around dusk my companions got one bear. It was a beautiful sunny day although the ice on our runners kept melting. We camped and fed our dogs. We will cache the load tomorrow. Back at our camp we talked and I tried to teach my companions about life, such as what would be good for white people and Eskimo people. I taught them again about the rules, that they should obey their leader and if they plan to work for a white man to be punctual so that they would not have to be embarrassed by him. They should not rest as much if they plan to work and to do their best at all times. I told them also that if they take something to make sure to tell the owner. This way they would attain the respect of the police, the store clerk and everybody else.

Tomorrow we will look for seals and bears. The weather is getting nice now. We are beginning to feel the warmth of the sun during the day.

N.W.T. Separates from Canada
Alootook Ipellie

The Inuit have developed a strong political consciousness in recent years. Inspired by the Quebec Separatist movement, Alootook Ipellie wrote this satire for Inuit Today *in 1977.*

What if one day in this century the above headline became a reality? We all know that it will never even come close to becoming true in this generation, and probably never will in the future. But what if it did become a reality? The following is a brief account of fictitious events that may have taken place on the day the proposed N.W.T. referendum on separation from Canada was announced.

The Nunavut government today announced the date of their referendum on the N.W.T. separation from the rest of Canada. In a surprise move that shocked the federal government and the people of Canada, the Nunavut government decided that a referendum would be held to find out whether the people of the North, the Inuit and non-Inuit, want to break away from the confines of Canada, and especially from the hands of the federal government which has for decades kept the Inuit from exercising their rights as free people. The Inuit say they have been treated as colonial subjects ever since the first white people moved to the North in the early 1900s.

The Inuit, spearheaded by their leaders, have for many years now protested the federal government's constant hold on their lives as though they were only little infant children whose mother had departed for the unknown. Pressure has been building up in the minds of many Inuit who have for so long been deprived of their right to govern their own people.

The exact date of the referendum will be August 30th of this year. That's about six months from now. You can be sure a lot of lobbying will be carried out by the Nunavut government before that time.

When one talks about the people of Canada being shocked to hear of the proposed referendum, that is only putting it mildly. The turn of events that took place today has hitherto been unheard of. No one, not even the majority of the people of the North itself, expected the news.

Inuit language being eroded
At a press conference held today, the premier of Nunavut, Nanookutaa Limaaq, said that his people have lived long enough without the right to learn their own language in the federally-run schools across the vast North. The schools, he said, were places where Inuit children willingly go each morning to learn the ways of the white culture without ever even hearing a single word of the Inuit language during the entire school year. This, he said, was not good enough for the Inuit, who have managed to hold on to their delicate traditions in spite of the tremendous barrage of white man's culture that has been invading every Inuit household in the North.

Quebecers said no
The N.W.T. referendum follows the unsuccessful Quebec referendum which was held last November 15th. Many people in Canada are still buzzing about the referendum for Quebec independence, which was defeated by a narrow margin. The Canadian people have spent the last three months recollecting themselves and are

34   *Alootook Ipellie*

much relieved that the people of Quebec have decided to remain Canadians. The mistaken belief of the Parti Québécois that the passing of time would convert enough followers to their side resulted in a great shock to them.

PET wants back

Former prime minister Pierre Elliott Trudeau, otherwise known as PET, has seen his now famous speech before the joint meeting of the U.S. Congress proven true. This was the speech in which he so eloquently said that "Separatism in Quebec is DEAD." Mr. Trudeau said today that he had been elated when he learned of the defeat of the Quebec referendum last November, and he expressed hope that the Inuit would also make the decision to remain in Canada. He said he believed Inuit were a group of people who would not allow themselves to break away from Canada, which he said has done a lot for them in the past. He predicted the Inuit would vote to remain Canadians as they always have. Mr. Trudeau also announced today that he will run for the leadership at the next Liberal Party convention to be held in Frobisher Bay, N.W.T. And if he becomes leader of the party, he predicted the Liberals would also win the next federal election which will be held early next summer.

"They will vote for independence"

Jonathon H.P.C. Koomakoolook, an expert on Inuit affairs, said he was not surprised by the proposed referendum. He said the Inuit have long been oppressed people who have waited decades for this referendum. He predicted the Inuit would vote to separate from Canada with a large margin, and in this way, finally get their wish to govern themselves. The federal government, he said, has neglected the wishes of the Inuit for many years, and there is no

Alootook Ipellie 35

question that the Inuit will get the right to strike back at the federal government for the mistakes it has made in running Inuit affairs in the past. Mr. Koomakoolook said the Inuit are capable of making great strides to better the condition of their people in a way the people of Canada never dreamed was possible. He said the Inuit will start to achieve great things within a few years of the referendum. "The federal government's failure to recognize the potential of the Inuit to govern themselves has made a lot of Inuit leaders perspire with rage. There will certainly be rejoicing among them the day of the referendum," Mr. Koomakoolook predicted.

Northerners speak out

The general reaction from the people of the North is mixed. Peeta Kudluk, chairman of the Igloolik community council, said he was thrilled to hear of the proposed referendum and said he believed there is a very good chance that the Inuit will vote to separate from Canada. He mentioned the deplorable condition the educational system is in and said it was about time things were starting to change in that department. The way education is carried out in the North is pure nonsense and would never be allowed to happen in the South by the white people, Mr. Kudluk said.

Ivialook Sooni, who is believed to be the oldest man now living in the North, took the news in his stride, but he expressed concern that this referendum may well work against his people in the long run. He said if the Inuit choose to separate from the rest of Canada at this time, it will create a mini chaos within the northern community as a whole. He feared for the lack of Inuit trained to run a new government in a separate state. Mr. Sooni said he hoped the referendum would be postponed for at least another five to ten years, so the Inuit would have enough time to prepare for when the N.W.T. becomes a separate state. He also pointed out that he

36   *Alootook Ipellie*

would welcome whole-heartedly a decision by the Inuit to separate. "It is about time we Inuit were given a chance to prove to the world that we have our own culture and a way of governing our own people that has never been tried in the North," he said. Mr. Sooni gave his people full points for having the courage to attempt such an enormous project that would shake up the North in a way that has never been seen in the whole history of Canada.

The local gathering spots throughout the communities in the North are ringing out with a sort of carnival atmosphere with people all talking about the proposed referendum.

Canada—his "homeland"

Pete "the provider" Brewer, a local bartender/manager in Inuvik, shouted out above the noisy customers: "The referendum is for me a little scary! I just can't imagine me and my family living under a separate state from the rest of Canada. Canada is my homeland, and I aim to remain a devoted Canadian as long as I stand on this earth! I look upon Canada as a saviour of human dignity and a symbol of freedom for mankind. It is sad that the Inuit may choose to leave it! Look, the government of Canada has done a ton of good for these poor creatures of the North! It has developed the North in a proper manner, in a humane way, and in the right way! It has helped a doomed people to survive the odds and kept them from becoming an extinct race! And it has brought health care to the Inuit and gotten rid of the pain that would have destroyed them forever! Just look at their lifestyle today compared to the days when they were nomads! Hasn't the government done a great job of rescuing them from imminent extinction from the face of the earth?! Well, anyway, the announcement of a referendum has certainly created a lot of excitement throughout the North and in this town! That kind of excitement brings good business for us!

Alootook Ipellie 37

People have something to talk about once again and there is no better place than a bar to go and sound out their views! Heh! Heh!"

It's their future
Illi Niakti, a senior student and the president of the student council at the Gordon Robertson Educational Centre in Frobisher Bay, said he was quite surprised by the proposed referendum. He said he was very optimistic about the referendum and welcomed it. It has been the general feeling among the young people of the North that it is about time the Inuit were given a fighting chance to run their own affairs. He said the young people have a lot at stake in this referendum and must not be counted out in any way. Mr. Niakti called for a vote for every student in the North regardless of their age because he said their very future will be decided upon in this referendum.

"If the young people are to be prevented from exercising their rights in this referendum," he said, "they might as well give the referendum to the dogs! We have had enough neglect from our elders, and especially from the government!"

Mr. Niakti volunteered to head a special section to look after the needs of the young people in the referendum and to manage their votes entirely separately from the main vote for the northern people.

It was as if the old man winter had come
The reaction of the N.W.T. council to the proposed referendum was not surprising. It was cold. With its reputation for being just another branch of the federal government bureaucracy, the N.W.T. council opposed the referendum with all its strength. Some members of the council just shook their heads without a word. Some refused to be interviewed. Others simply said: "It's Commu-

nism!" "It's outright madness on the part of the Inuit!" "A sad day for all of Canada to endure."

His taste was simply sour

The commissioner of the council, Mr. Govern Bullman, reacted with some bitterness toward the Inuit leaders for thinking up such a storm that was not even wanted by the people. "The proposed referendum is all part of the Parti Québécois' plan to take over the N.W.T. as soon as the Inuit vote to separate from Canada. Their loss in the Quebec referendum was a blow to them, and now the N.W.T. referendum gives them their second chance to go for separation," he said. Mr. Bullman expressed fear that the Quebec government would take over the N.W.T. the same day the Inuit vote to separate.

Minister goes into hibernation

Department of Indian and Northern Affairs Minister Buddy Boss could not be reached for his reaction. He was rumoured to be in his little hideout somewhere in the Gatineau Hills across the Ottawa River from the Parliament Buildings. The report said that he was deep into his 'think' session about the referendum. He had last been seen storming out of his Ottawa office, and with reporters clawing at him, he was heard to have said two words: "It's rubbish!" That was the last of him. It will be extremely interesting to hear what he has to say about the proposed referendum on separation when he finally comes out of his brief hibernation.

It's their chance to be "captain"

For many northerners, especially the Inuit, the referendum will mean a chance to take command of their own "ship". For the other residents now living in the North, who are not of Inuit origin, it's a

Alootook Ipellie 39

time of uncertainty. They will have to decide whether to stay in the N.W.T., or bail out if the people of the North should decide to separate from Canada. There is evidence that most non-Inuit are sympathetic toward the native people and hope that they will some day be given a chance to run their own lives. But many of the non-Inuit are already talking about "the big move south to Canada" if the N.W.T. should separate.

Only time will tell if the Inuit want to remain Canadians or become independent.

For the second time in history, all of Canada and the world is once again sitting back and waiting to see if a group of people within Canada, this time the Inuit, will move to split away and form their own homeland where they will have the right to govern their own people.

Will separatism break up Canada this time around? We shall know the answer to this important question on August 30th.

Land
John Weetaltuk

John Weetaltuk has written a number of articles pleading for a more sensitive attitude towards the environment. If this piece has an Old Testament ring to it, it is because the Bible has been read in syllabics and roman orthography in many camps and settlements across the Arctic for over a hundred years and is familiar to even the smallest Eskimo child. This essay comes from Inukshuk, *January 1976.*

We the living arise every morning to greet a new day. We rise to see sun, clouds or rain and yet snow is always welcome to those who live with it. There over the horizon, from the east the sun climbs over the hills of beautiful orange and red. We look at the sun, the sky, the clouds and figure out what the day will be. Even though we look into the far off space we forget that there is something between the skies and beautiful weather.

Twenty-four hours a day it turns, it changes, it grows and it's solid. How many of us remember where we were born, or how many of us remember a special area that things took place? How many of us remember the vast and unspoiled land that used to be?

Land, God-made, ingenious planet we live in, as distinguished from other heavenly bodies, or from the dwelling place of spirits. We, the prisoners of the earth, of whatever size, shape or form we are, all live and die, be we man, beast or fowl; we have to share the planet.

Generation upon generations the land we live in never seems to change; we rise to see the glory of the skies, the setting of another

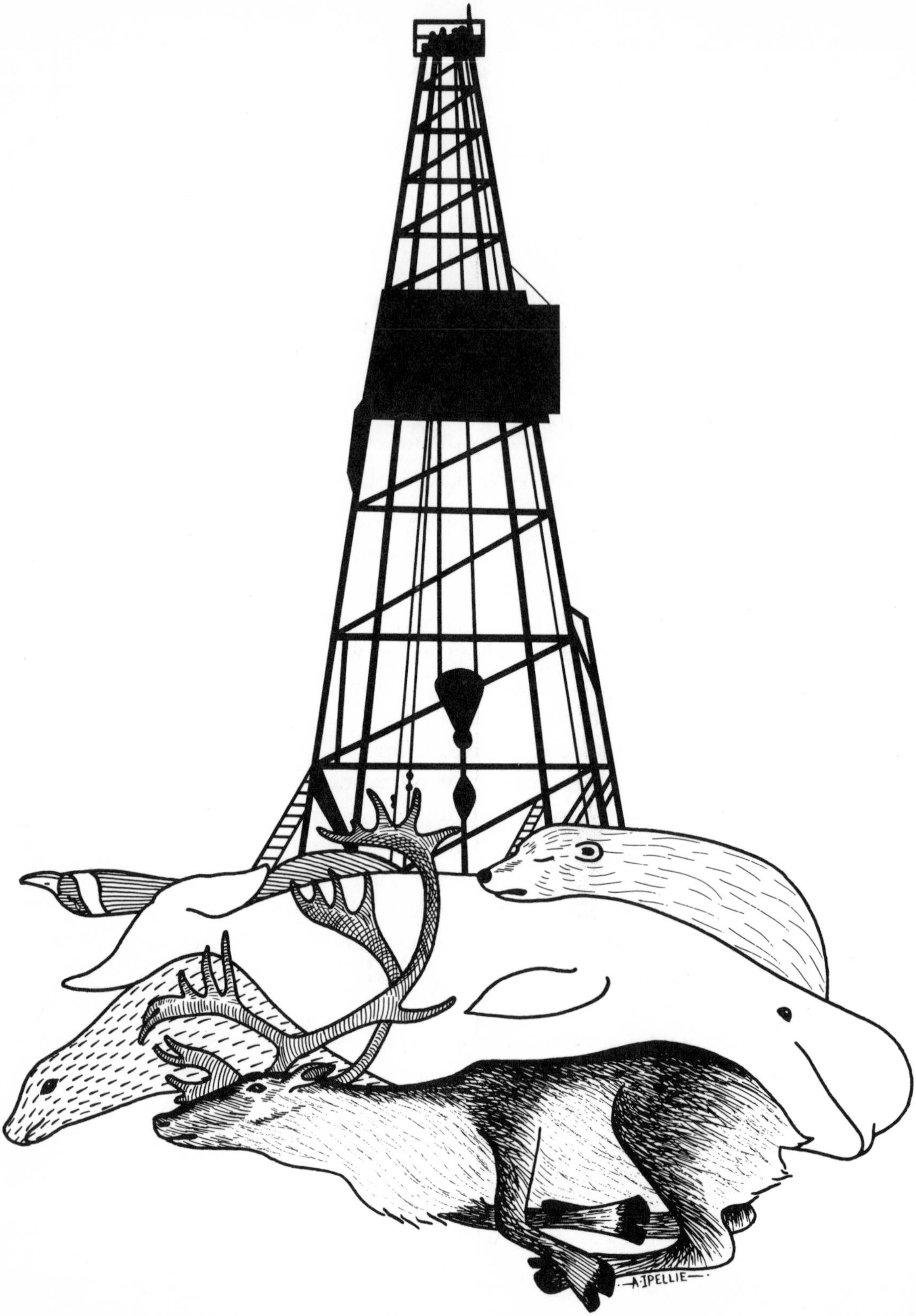
A. IPELLIE

day, and yet this land that is on our feet is there. Take it away, where would be the joy of living?

Land claims, who, where and how? Behold the birds do claim areas of their own, behold the beast they too seek land, now put man into it, which of the three gains more land.

It is a shame to take the land where birds may mate and lay eggs, it is also a disgrace to keep on pushing the beast until there is no more feeding grounds. Why gas, why oil? Why roads and why this and why that? Our forefathers have lived through it. Our children's next children will ask: "Were there such animals and birds?" Even now there are birds and animals completely extinct. Generation upon generations man killed and man died. All corners of the earth you'll find where blood had been spilled. Why? Is the earth too small? Is the earth not good enough? Or is the earth too good? Those of you who look into land claims there is guilt if our land is destroyed. I don't think anyone needs fifteen acres to turn around.

So You Want to Kill an Eskimo
Anthony Apakark Thrasher

Tony Thrasher was convicted of manslaughter for beating a man to death in a Calgary rooming house. He was sentenced to seven years in prison. While there, he wrote down his memories of his childhood and the chain of events that led from the western Arctic to a British Columbia federal penitentiary via a drunken brawl in a Calgary bar. This extract from his book Skid Row Eskimo, *which was published in 1976, describes events that followed his involvement in a prison riot.*

Even the summer breezes knew enough to stay out of Prince Albert Penitentiary.

More than once during August I almost collapsed from the heat. The cellblock was like the devil's furnace. My sweat soaked clear through my cheap, canvas prison outfit. Though I'd only see the sun when they'd let me out into the exercise yard each evening from six to nine-thirty, its energy crept into every room, locked in by the same high walls that kept everybody else inside that prison.

Whenever I got the chance, I'd sneak into the meat cooler in the kitchen. It was nice in there. But they kicked me out when they caught me. Other than the meat cooler, there was no place to escape. At night, the cellblock was impossible to sleep in. My bedding was wet. So was everybody else's. Even the cracked plaster of our cells was sweating. You could see drops of water streaking down from the ceiling.

The long, unbroken days of temperatures in the eighties were beginning to get to guys' minds in there.

More and more often you could hear screams in the night. Guys going crazy in their cells, stir crazy. They'd scream for a long time. Then you'd just hear muffled sobbing.

The guards, patrolling silently along the landing, seemed to sense the tension. Through the bars of my cell I could see that they were more alert, their faces drawn, their eyes flicking from cell to cell.

Then it happened.

A nigger guy slashed an Indian with a knife.

The effect on the exercise yard that evening was explosive. All the white guys and niggers began grouping together on one side of the yard, the Indians and half-breeds on the other. They were getting set for a big brawl and it wasn't long in coming.

Somebody shouted that two niggers were cornered in the gym. It was all anybody needed.

A big gang of Indians ran from the yard toward the gym, with a gang of white guys and niggers in hot pursuit. I followed behind, and when I neared the gym I could see a full-scale riot had broken out.

Furniture was being smashed and blood from bashed noses was all over the place. I couldn't hear myself think for the screaming and shouting and thumping going on, so I figured I'd better get in there and help somebody.

I ripped off a table leg and went in swinging. When I saw more than two guys ganging up on a friend, I just put my stick in between them and broke it up. Soon guards began popping up here and there and guys were being dragged back to their cells to cool off. Within half an hour, it was all over. We were locked in our cells, none the worse for wear except for a few guys who got black eyes and busted noses.

That riot taught me something—the need to have a knife

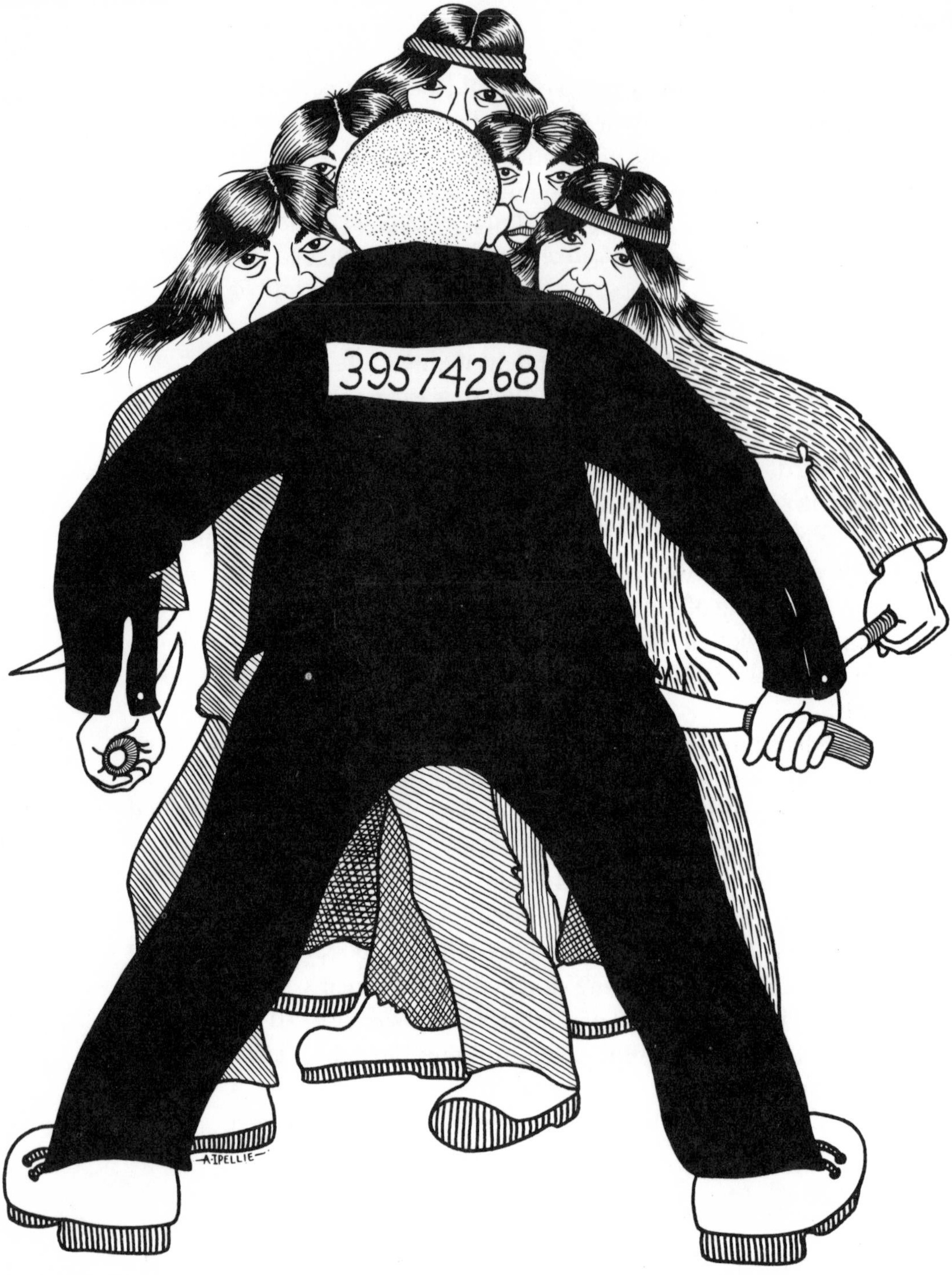
39574268
A.IPELLIE

handy. I saw knives among some of the men in the gym. A lot of inmates seemed to have them hidden in their cells. I figured I'd better get myself one.

On a trip to the kitchen I grabbed a carving knife. To tell you the truth, I grabbed two. I had no trouble getting by the guards with the knives tucked under my shirt. They seemed to trust me a lot. I guess it was because I never gave them trouble as other inmates did.

That week, those knives saved my life.

It was a quiet afternoon and I was dozing in my cell after finishing some school work. It must have been my hunter's instinct. There wasn't exactly a sound, but I was suddenly aware of some action behind me.

Without giving it a second thought, I sprang from my cot and faced the door.

Standing there were five big Indians.

"White-lover," the tall one said quietly, so the guards couldn't hear. I could see the steel glinting in his clenched fist. The others had them, too. Cell-sharpened table knives.

They said they were going to kill me because I took the side of the whites in the riot. I had never heard of such silly business. All I'd done was keep some guys from being smashed up. But I wasn't going to stand there and argue with them.

I could smell something on their breath, and their eyes were glassy. I guessed it was extract from the kitchen. They didn't seem too steady on their feet and I figured, in their drunken state, I could probably move quicker than they could.

Bounding to the rear of my cell, I grabbed up my carving knives, one in each hand. Those Indians didn't have a chance to get to me.

Anthony Apakark Thrasher 47

"Okay, you heroes," I said, crouched, ready to spring. "So you want to murder an Eskimo. Let's see you try . . ."

I've skinned a lot of animals in my life. Those five animals, I figured, I could skin them easy enough, too.

"Well . . . what do you say?"

They didn't say anything. They were too busy staring at my two big meat cutters to answer. It was enough for them. They turned and fled back to their cellblock. I never had any trouble with them after that.

Song Composed for the Visit of Their Excellencies Governor General and Mrs. Mitchener to Igloolik, Mayday 1969
François Tamnaruluk

In the old days, songs were frequently composed spontaneously to celebrate the occurrence of some special event. The visit of Queen Elizabeth's representative to an Arctic community in 1969 was sufficiently important to revive the tradition. Tamnaruluk's song was printed in the Igloolik newspaper, Midnight Sun.

Happiness is here
I found the song,
Ai - ai - ai.

48   *François Tamnaruluk*

People's happiness
Is not to be forgotten,
Ai - ai - ai.

This song wants to go away
So I'll tie it into my throat,
Ai - ai - ai.

It really wants to go
It wants to go to the future,
Ai - ai - ai.

It looks as if
It knows the drum,
Ai - ai - ai.

This song is not too good
But it will be a good song
Along with the drum,
Ai - ai - ai.

This song is sometimes mixed-up
With the words,
Ai - ai - ai

The end is coming
We are running out of words,
Ai - ai - ai

François Tamnaruluk 49

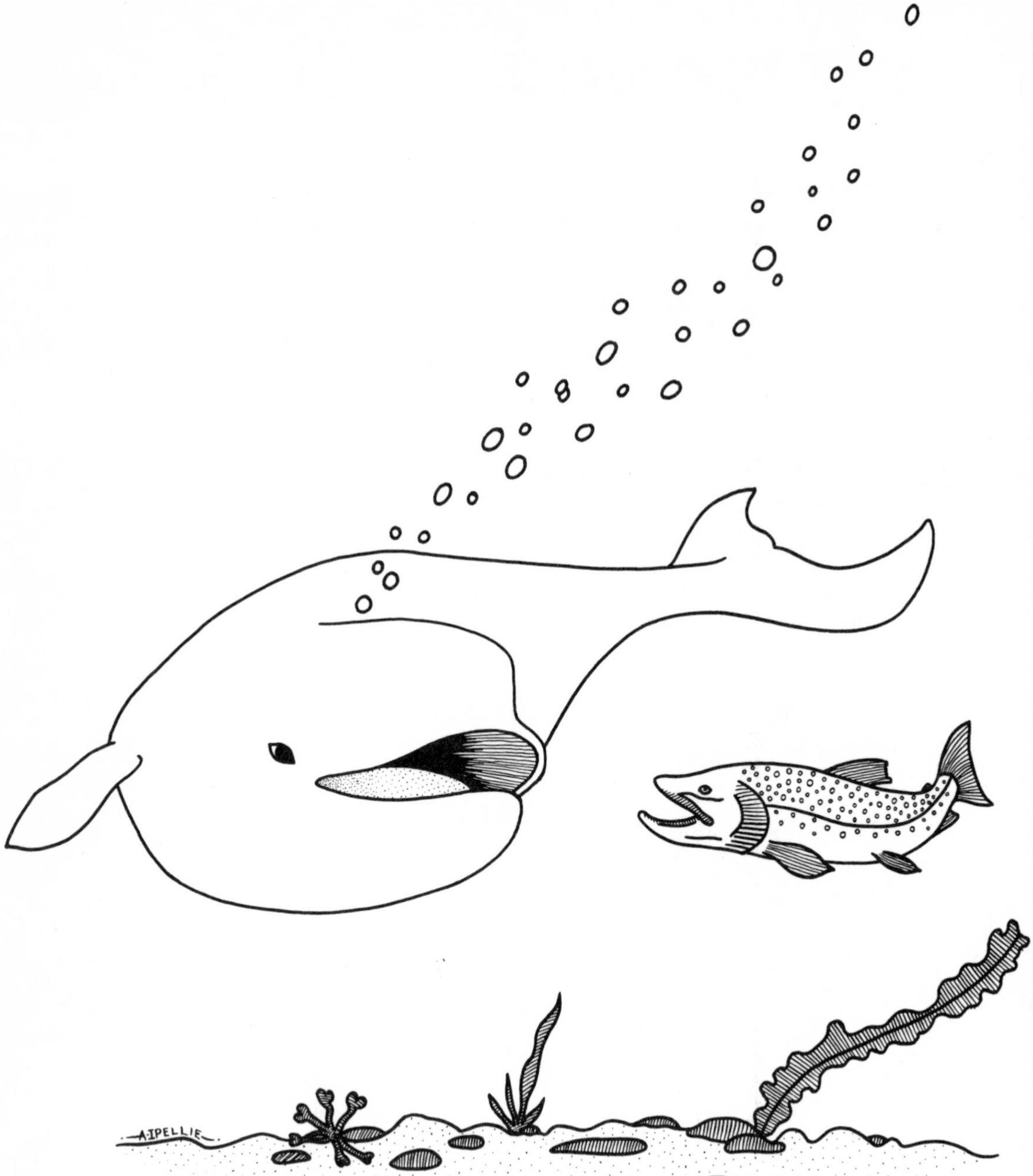
A.IPELLIE

The Whale and the Char
Anonymous

A good translator can make a major contribution to a story, just as a bad one can destroy even the most brilliant work. In this story, first published in Inuktitut *in 1972, there are two artists evident: the storyteller who composed the narrative and the translator who caught the tone of his low-key humour. Both these artists have remained anonymous.*

Once a giant whale was laying in the open water between the shore and the pack ice. With his back above the water, he looked like a big island. He was feeding on the delicious plankton that came floating by when, suddenly, something big bumped hard against his lips and frightened him. He turned over with a mighty flip of his tail that sent a high wave crashing against the shore. When the whale discovered that it was only a char that had struck him, he began to laugh.

"Why should I, the largest beast in the world, be frightened by a little char?" he said aloud.

The char heard him and was very angry because he did not like to be called "little". He was, after all, larger than a trout, or a herring or a whitefish.

"What a clumsy animal you are!" shouted the char. He shouted right into the whale's ear, which was very bad manners.

The whale now became angry because he did not like to be called "clumsy". The two began to argue and shout insults at each other.

"What good are you anyway?" said the char at last. "It is well known that people prefer me over all the other fish in the water."

"But you are hardly a meal for one family," answered the whale. "When people catch me, I am big enough to feed a whole settlement for a year."

"But it takes many strong men with harpoons and boats to catch you and sometimes you kill the hunters with your tail. You are a dangerous animal."

The whale was very proud of his strength and he made his chest bigger because everything the char said was true.

"I am more useful to people than you are," said the char. "You cannot live under the ice in winter. I am close by in all seasons and even old women and children can catch me when they are hungry. I never let people starve."

The whale again knew that all the char said was true. He blew up a high spout of water as his chest deflated and then he swam far out to sea to hide his shame. That is all.

The Story of John Ayaruaq
John Ayaruaq

The autobiography of John Ayaruaq was the first book to be published entirely in Eskimo syllabics. The first chapter was translated and printed in English in several magazines. Ayaruaq, of Rankin Inlet, is well known among the people of the west coast of the Hudson Bay for his folk tales, but in these opening pages of his book he tells about his childhood and a dreadful catastrophe that occurred. The piece, first published in Intercom, *is taken from* North, *March 1969.*

John Ayaruaq is going to tell a story.

My father's name was Uvinik and my mother's was Iquaq. My father had two wives, Iquaq and Haakuluk, and Iquaq was my real mother. I was the only son in the whole family and loved by all of them very much. My father and Haakuluk gave me more attention and of course my mother loved me but not as strongly as my father and Haakuluk. Haakuluk also had an adopted son.

I also remember my father's mother who was blind. Her name was Ipirqaq. My father had mixed feelings of hate and love towards her.

When I was three years old, I remember travelling to Qatitta-lik, maybe around the middle of July, with my father and mother and my sister, Quguliq. We were quite a few in a boat—twelve of us. And there were ten passengers in another boat, travelling with us.

Now we were on a little island which is at the mouth of Ukkusissalik. We put up a camp there as we were unable to travel because of the ice breaking up. I think we stayed there many days. I remember gathering wood on the island and Nanauq, Maniq's wife, went with us. She walked on the ice; suddenly she got carried away on the floe and we could hear her crying but she was rescued.

While we were still on the island there was a seal sun-bathing on the ice and my father shot it. He didn't even get close to it, just shot it from the island. He didn't even bother to get the seal but left it on the ice. Kanguq, Sissaaq and Ikkitinnuaq went and got the seal and ate it. My father did not eat with them because he knew (through his power as a shaman) that the seal was not real so he did not eat with the others.

Because there was no route to Qattitalik we decided to return to Repulse Bay. Two boats were on their way back, ours and Mirquirsinilik's. Then while we were crossing Ukkusissalik we found out there was no route on account of the pack of ice. When we reached the shore we were not able to get on the land so we had to go through two pieces of ice to land because the ice was hard to move to make our way. Taqaugaq went to see if he could find a way to open water, while the women went by the side of the boat to relieve themselves. I remember that there were four of us in the boat at that moment, and that I was looking at rocks and seaweeds moving with the motion of water at the bottom of the sea.

Suddenly the ice, moved by the currents of the water, fell on the boats and destroyed them. And all we could see was the sail pole, and the rear of one of the boats. Shortly after, both of them disappeared. A father and a son, Ikkitinnuaq and Igunaassiaq, were killed. We could also see Haakuluk holding on to her adopted child in the midst of smacking ice. My father, Taquagaq, Kanguq and Sammurtuq tried to get hold of her but it was difficult because of the moving ice. Finally they reached Haakuluk. I came up right beside my little sister and when I saw her I recognized her. I had one foot on a piece of ice and this I will never forget, although I was

maybe three years old when this happened. While I was floating on
the piece of ice I could see others gathered around Haakuluk who
was dying. They reached her adopted child who was still alive but
all torn and broken bones. But my real mother, Iquaq, was gone!
The others told me that my mother jumped back in the water on
purpose when she couldn't see me and her body was never seen but
her intestines floated with the motion of water and ice. And a voice
could be heard under the ice and we could not move the ice to
search for the person and it was pathetic! And we lost all our
belongings.

After the ice had calmed down we saw Angutimmarik and his
family coming back in his boat. When they saw us and realized
what had happened they hurried (but not as fast as they would

John Ayaruaq 55

have with a motor), battling and paddling as fast as they could. First they just went by us to the island and left some passengers behind; then they came back and got us. I don't remember being frightened when they arrived. But we could still hear a voice underneath the ice. They broke the ice with an axe and there was Sissaaq, his hip all ruined, and two others who were brought to land and both dying.

Because of the taboo, Haakuluk's body was left on the ice for I don't know how many days, and it was awful to see it lying on the ice. Five people died and five got badly hurt, my father, Kanguq, Taqaugaq, Sammurtuq and myself. My eyes went out of place and I was told they were red.

We stayed on the island maybe five days to mourn. After the five days we continued our journey and the ones that were not hurt badly walked by the shore and the others went by boat. Whenever they had to cross a river they came into the boat, because they knew which rivers were hard to cross by foot. Then I felt frightened because my father began to have a reaction from the shock while he was still in the boat; it was caused by grief and pain of his broken leg, but mostly from losing his two wives. They were fighting and crying in the boat trying to calm him down and to save him from killing himself. That was the episode that frightened me most. I often talk about this, but this is the first time I have written it down in detail.

Wonderful Life
Leah Idlout

This essay strongly resembles the traditional story of "The Many Lives of Anakajuttuq" by Joe Panipakuttuk, which describes how a soul inhabits various objects and animals until it comes to rest in a human body. Here, Leah Idlout uses the old Inuit theme to express the self-assurance and confidence she developed as an adult. The essay is from Inuit Today, *November 1975.*

I wish I was a paper so everyone can see me or read me all over and keep me with them and understand me in their own kind of language with their own kind of taste and feeling. No! My dear, I can be a cloud instead, way up in the sky where I can see you first, then everyone and go everywhere with all kinds of colors: hanging low or high, in the North, South, West or East, just anywhere I can be cold and warm, blue or clean, even when I am anywhere in the World, I can be nothing else a cloud, cloud, cloud. But, when clouds are crying the people won't like it for me to cry for them; so I wish I was a big moon with a big, big, smiling face that everyone can see. But, the moon is always changing into different forms, even when it makes the sky beautiful. But I would only appear during the evening with a wide smiling face, so I wish I was a sun who is keeping warm and making everybody warm too at the same time. But, the people would always ask me to keep shining and keep them warm and when it is getting too hot for them, they would look for something to cover themselves from me or to hide from me where they can have more fun without me. So I wish I was a star, but I don't know which one, maybe to be better than any other star. So I wish I was a tree, but trees don't move around at all to go with the others. So I wish I was an animal so the people can choose me to be their kind of a pet which is me. But I would be bought too expensive and I would not be able to talk with you at all, I would not be able to help you with anything much, but to keep you too proud of me. I am going to be a flower, but the flowers are too pretty and die young like I may. WHAT CAN I BE? Well, I guess I am going to be just what I am, that is to be myself, as a human being, and to have fun whenever I want to with my good kind of friends and have good fun and to be truly loving like—you, and to cry whenever I feel like it; laugh in my own way with you, and be very happy when you are or sad when you are sad; or mad when you are mad, and to see my kind at night or at daytime as your kind. Being a human being is fun, when you are enjoying your short life that the creator created. Every human being was created by one only, so one may see the day and night of the world where our land is, and to hear, to feel and to see years, days, hours, minutes, seconds go by as the warm and cold years go by. You can do many good things in your own life like mine. You already have done so many good things that you haven't realized or thought of, BECAUSE the life is busy and full of fun. Make your life happy and for the others too.

The Custom
Charlie Patsauq

*In this story, written when he was a teenager at the high school in
Frobisher Bay, Patsauq sensitively expresses his understanding of
one of the grim traditions formerly practised by his people in their
struggle to survive. The story is taken from the newspaper*
Inukshuk, *June 1974.*

The old man was becoming useless to his sons. He was now
becoming a burden to them. Just an old man, another mouth to
feed. Useless weight when he sat on the sled as the dogs pulled. The
village was slowly starving, this was the time of famine for the
Eskimos. The hunters were now deciding where to go. The old
man knew it was up to his sons whether or not he was to be left
behind. He knew there were many reasons for him to be abandoned when the village moved as was the custom when old people
became useless. Recently when other people began to talk of
moving to other hunting grounds, his sons became less talkative,
the old man knew what they were thinking about, abandon or take
him?

The day came to move. There were few dogs, the majority of
the dogs had died of starvation. The dead dogs had been fed to the
other dogs to keep them alive. The people, too, had eaten the dead
dogs in desperation. It was time to move. The sons loaded their
sled with only the essentials. Then they came inside the igloo and
sat beside the old man.

The older son spoke first, "Father, we love and respect you very much but we will have to leave you behind. We would unhesitatingly stay here and die with you but the people need us. Many hunters have died during this great hunger, so the people need as many hunters as possible. Please understand, father."

"I understand, I have been anticipating this. Leave me behind, leave with my blessings," said the old man.

"Father," said the older son, "how do you want to die? Do you want us to hang you, or do you want to die by my harpoon or should we just leave you behind to starve to death?"

"Hang me, my dear sons, I command you to do it."

The sons slowly went up and put a hole in the top of the igloo and put a sealskin rope through it. They formed a noose and put it on the old man's neck after they had let him stand on a snow block a foot high from the ground. Neither of the sons could bring themselves to kick the block away. Then the younger son brought up his courage, "I will kick the block away," he said to his father and brother. His brother left the igloo and went outside.

The son said to his father, "Forgive me, father, but I must do it."

"There is nothing to forgive, my son, it is the way of our people."

The younger son started crying but he kicked the block from under the old man's feet. His father did not struggle. The young son was now on his knees crying openly. His elder brother walked in with the rest of the people who had anticipated the whole thing. The people understood why they had done it and they comforted the brothers. Then they went to their dogs and started moving out, with the brothers leading, both brothers weeping with grief.

One of Those Wonderful Nights
Alootook Ipellie

Alootook Ipellie is one of the most prolific contemporary Inuit journalists. His stories, poems and articles have appeared in North, Inuktitut, Inukshuk *and* Tukisiviksat. *He is also the principal writer for* Inuit Today, *in which this poem was published in April 1974. Ipellie grew up in the settlement of Frobisher Bay, but in his poems he often seems to have lived the old, nomadic camp life of his grandfather.*

It was one of those wonderful nights
When we gathered at the dance house.
I recall the familiar sights
When everyone laughed and danced
And had a tremendous time.
The great drums were booming,
Hands were clapping,
And happy faces were rocking back
And forth with the rhythmic dancing
Of the woman who had four legs.
Happy were those days when this
Woman danced all night long without
Resting for a moment.
She gave us so much joy,
So much feeling for life,
That the hazards of the land were
Forgotten—
On one of those wonderful nights
When we gathered at the dance house.

The First Religious Time
Peter Pitseolak

Peter Pitseolak is sometimes called the historian of Baffin Island. In the 1940s he taught himself photography, sometimes developing pictures in an igloo warmed only with a stone lamp, using a flashlight covered with red "kadluna" material. Throughout his adult life he kept a syllabic diary, and at the age of seventy-one he wrote the recent history of his people in Cape Dorset. This is an extract from the oral biography that accompanies that manuscript in People from Our Side, *by Peter Pitseolak and Dorothy Eber.*

I was born when Christianity had already come to Baffin Island. For myself, I did not like the old, old way because the shamans would kill the people they did not like. When the ministers came the shamans stopped their killings. Reverend Peck—Okhamuk—was the first minister to bring the word of God to Baffin Island. People were very fond of him because he was so loving with all the people and very friendly.

Even before I was able to talk I had learned all the alphabet songs by listening to people sing them. Okhamuk taught the people the alphabets by singing. When the government had come to the North and they were handing out these papers with the Eskimo alphabet and the English alphabet, a man came and said, "You have to learn these." I told him, "I knew them before I could talk." He said, "You can't possibly know these," and I said, "What do you want me to do? Close my eyes and sing them to you?" He was very surprised that I knew them in both languages. He said, "So you have learned."

But at that time, when the people were changing, they believed the wrong things. They were so mixed up they overdid their religion. The first religious time took place in 1901, the year before I was born. When you tell a story about these people who were overdoing their religion it sounds as if they were all drunk. They were blind to what they were doing.

I'll start at the beginning. Simigak was out hunting one night, sitting by the seal hole waiting for a seal to come up. All of a sudden he saw Jesus coming down to watch him. He thought it was Jesus but he was mistaken; it was Satan. When he returned home he told the people he had seen Jesus. Then Simigak said, "We must get together, everybody must get together," and they all went to a place near Cape Dorset called Tooneen. There they built a giant igloo for a church. It had no roof so they could see the Heavens.

Simigak was the chief in the Etidliajuk area—I've heard he was the tallest man in Seekooseelak—and he was in charge. But when they gathered in the big new church, Simigak's cousin, Keegak, was outdoing everyone with the ceremony. In that church the leadership passed to Keegak—'the messenger', that was the meaning of his name. He became the leader because he strongly believed that Simigak had seen Jesus. He thought of a Keegak as a person who was looking after all the people like a God. Keegak was the God in the first religious time.

In the giant igloo the people gathered to worship. Keegak was dancing and singing. He led the dances and he sang:

I am, I am, I am,
I am the big God,
God thinks of me.
I am
There in Sugluk,

There in Padlee,
I am, here I am.
I am, eee iii, eeii, eee
I am here; I am.

Once he danced naked. He was a saint now and he no longer had any sins. He was dancing wildly. His male organs were swinging all over the place. His belly had red marks from dancing so wildly. He danced and danced. But the igloo had no roof and finally he began to get cold. Then he said, "I am going to Heaven! I am going up; I am going up." He told everyone to get out of the igloo. "Everybody out; everybody out." People were confused about what was going on. They began to get out. Inukjuarjuk was the last person to start to leave but when he was going Keegak stopped him. "We are both going up," he said. He said this because he had borrowed Annie, Inukjuarjuk's daughter.

But Simigak didn't like the idea that only two people should go to Heaven, and he said, "You are not the only ones who are going up; you are not the only ones going up. We are all going up."

Of course nobody got up. Finally Keegak had to go home because he got too cold. His penis had goose pimples.

After this, whenever Evitah, Keegak's daughter, went to visit people they used to ask her, "Has your father gone up yet?" She used to answer, "No. Because the Eskimo people have too many sins."

Keegak was singing in the igloo all the time. He sang that the same things were happening in other places. He saw that Sugluk people in Arctic Quebec and Padluk people around Pangnirtung had the same things going on. People thought Keegak had become a shaman because he could see what was happening in other places.

64   *Peter Pitseolak*

While the people were like this, they appointed a special person to cut the women's hair and shave the beards. Too much hair would drag people back when they were going up. The women had cold heads! And Martha, Keegak's wife, would chew on the blubber and put blubber oil all over the clothing, especially on the new clothing. She'd say, "You're too neat; you're too neat." Pretty soon Martha and Keegak were the only people who had good clothing.

This happened after Okhamuk—Reverend Peck—had preached to the people that they should not be so possessive of their things. The people had seen Okhamuk and a few—only a few for at this time they were just starting to learn syllabics—had learned to read the Bible. There's a story about a man who was prideful of his possessions. All his clothing was in bright colours. They did not wish to be like him. A person like that could never be saved. So the people threw away all their good clothing and anything they had—rifles and beads. They kept their bad clothing and tried to have good hearts.

People even threw away their food. Anything Keegak asked for he would get. My father, Inukjuarjuk, had brought back from Quebec a plate—it had birds on it. Keegak asked for this plate and Kooyoo, my mother, was too quick to give it to him. She was afraid. Inukjuarjuk was not very pleased about this. "Why did you give that to him?" he asked.

People said Keegak was just like a white man—bossing everybody. All the other camps would bring him meat and he even had women who were not married to him making him clothes. He was a big boss now and he had a white man's jacket made out of sealskin.

Martha and Keegak had never been powerful but, all of a sudden, power was waiting for them. They grabbed it.

Peter Pitseolak   65

In the first religious time when Keegak became a Christian nobody was killed in our land although around Pangnirtung there was a killing at this time. There were no killings here but I think Keegak and Martha may have been trying to kill someone. In that giant igloo where they used to sing Keegak and Martha beat up two people. They were out of their minds, like white or Eskimo people when they are drunk. Keegak was jumping on the front side of a man who was lying on the ground. Martha was doing the same to a woman. The man's son told Keegak to stop jumping on his father so the man didn't die. This man was on the ground because he wasn't supposed to refuse if Keegak told him to do something. People were thinking that when Jesus was crucified he wasn't fighting back. So this man didn't fight back. No doubt he was trying to copy Jesus.

But even then they knew they were making mistakes. Simigak, Keegak's cousin, told him that only my father, Inukjuarjuk, and Simigak himself would be going to heaven because everyone else was making too many mistakes to get up. Keegak realized then he was wrong and said, "We're going to go along with you."

So Keegak wasn't a Keegak—the leader—any more. When he realized his name was wrong he wanted to go back to his old Inuit name, Annoyak. Then he took his baptized name, Jayko. He was really a friendly person. Most of the people liked him. He wasn't good looking but he had a good personality. He did some wrong but he was really a good person at the time he died. . . always trying to help with food. He died in 1923 and he is buried down in Etidliajuk in one of the two big barrels left by a ship.

One year after the first religious time, I would be born.

Ross Meets the Netchiliks
Ohokto

Sir John Ross's account of his first meeting with the Inuit of the Boothia was published and read by people all over the English-speaking world a hundred and fifty years ago. Inuit were impressed by the meeting too and, even though they had no way of writing down their version of the incident, it survived in the oral tradition and was recorded and published by L.A. Learmonth in 1948 in The Beaver.

On a day in the middle of the winter many years ago, off the north shore of Lord Mayor Bay, south Boothia, in the opening between what is now known as Victory Harbour and Felix Harbour, a number of Boothian (Netchilik) natives were out aglo hunting [breathing-hole sealing] as was their habit, when one, Ableelooktook, wandered far to the south of where his companions were hunting, led by his hunting dog straining eagerly at its leash. In permitting the dog to lead him there, Ableelooktook believed the animal had scented a bear. But suddenly he pulled up short because what was that he saw ahead?—strange sight indeed—what appeared to be a house, but not such as he was familiar with, with smoke pouring from its roof and many human beings moving around in its vicinity.

Not knowing what this strange sight could mean, Ableelooktook was greatly frightened, and without delay took to his heels and made back to the snow village, situated well back in the bay, whose entrance lay between Felix and Victory Harbours. There he arrived as darkness set in, and just as his companions also returned from their hunting.

Soon he had told of his discovery, upon which the whole population of the village quickly gathered together in the large village dance house to discuss the matter. Here the principal Angekok [medicine man] donned his main belt of charms and his cape, made of pieces of white deer belly hide, and without delay got to work. He first took a large deerskin and pegged it to the west wall inside the dance house so as to leave the lower side resting partly on the floor. He then obtained a pair of deerskin pants from one of the men and carefully laid them out on the floor behind the deerskin curtain with legs pointing towards the back wall, then crawled in behind the curtain, ordered all kudlik [stone lamp] lights to be extinguished, and the seance was on.

In crawling in behind the curtain the Angekok was careful to follow the direction travelled by the sun and the moon, because they were all afraid, and only thus could contact be established with the spirits it was necessary to consult. To have crawled in behind the curtain in the opposite direction to that travelled by the sun and the moon would have offended the spirits and prevented them from coming to the aid of these sorely troubled people.

As the crowd of scared men, women and children huddled together and anxiously waited in the darkened dance house, the Angekok got in touch with his familiar spirits and through them with all the other spirits that mattered, who all trooped in behind the curtain one after the other. First came those of the Sun, Moon and stars, then that of the giant who lived in the mountains back of Pelly Bay, of Nulaiyuk who controls the spirits of the mammals of the sea, of the deer and the bear and so on, down to even that of the lowly tom cod!

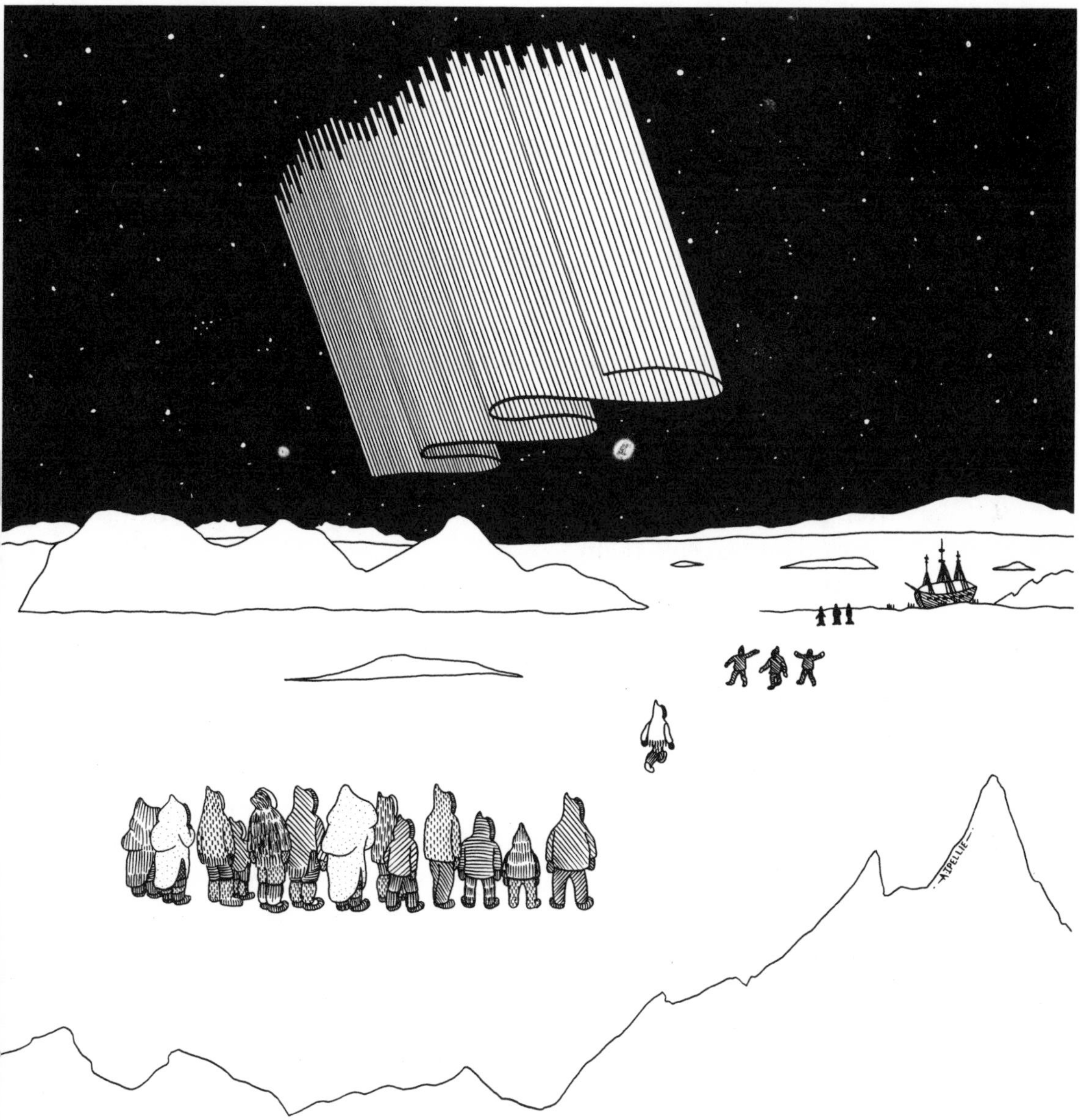
A.J.PELLIE

When all the spirits had gathered together under the curtain, they informed the Angekok that the strangers seen by Ableelooktook were white men and that they would welcome a visit by the Eskimos. Then to wind up, the spirits of the white men themselves arrived behind the curtain and invited all the Eskimos to visit their camp at Felix Harbour the following day.

Thus it was the entire population of the village turned out by daybreak the following morning and proceeded to Felix Harbour. When they came in sight of the house [the *Victory* under canvas covers and dismantled] they halted and sent forward Nalungituk to await the arrival of some of the white men who could be seen approaching without knives or spears or anything in their hands. Soon they were all on friendly terms with each other and moved over close to the house, where the boss of the white men came forward and greeted them.

After the second round of greeting was over, the boss [John Ross, presumably] enquired for the man who had been seen near the camp on the previous day as he wished to make him a present. Whereupon Ableelooktook stepped forward and went with him into the house. Once inside the boss handed him an ooloo, a woman's knife, which offended Ableelooktook, because he was a man and a great hunter. What did he want with a woman's knife? So he pointed to a hand saw which was hanging on a nail and indicated he would prefer that to the ooloo. This in turn made the boss angry, and he thereupon took the ooloo back from Ableelooktook, refused him the saw and chased him out of the house.

Afterwards the white men made presents of what appears to have been gun caps and what the Eskimos thought must be very small thimbles, and bullets which they afterwards used as sinkers for their fish jigging hooks, and thus ends the story of "Ableelooktook" as told by Ohokto.

70 *Ohokto*

The Giant Bear
Kiakshuk

To cope with the harsh Arctic environment in which they live, the Inuit have developed a sense of humour which sometimes borders on the grotesque. Their ability to laugh in the face of death has given them the ability to wait patiently through times of hunger, and to feast and enjoy themselves when the danger is past.

There once was a giant bear
who followed people for his prey.
He was so big he swallowed them whole:
Then they smothered to death inside him
if they hadn't already died of fright.

Either the bear attacked them on the run,
or if they crawled into a cave
where he could not squeeze his enormous body in,
he stabbed them with his whiskers like toothpicks,
drawing them out one by one,
and gulped them down.

No one knew what to do
until a wise man went out and let the bear swallow him,
sliding right down his throat into the big, dark, hot, slimy
    stomach.
And once inside there, he took his knife
and simply cut him open,
killing him of course.

He carved a door in the bear's belly
and threw out those who had been eaten before,
and then he stepped out himself
and went home to get help with the butchering.

Everyone lived on bear meat for a long time.
That's the way it goes:
Monster one minute, food the next.

Marble Island
Leonie Kappi

Leonie Kappi, who edited the book Northern People, *was born in Chesterfield Inlet, about sixty-five miles north of Rankin Inlet on Hudson Bay. She recorded this story for* North *in 1971 when she was working as a stenographer for the Territorial government.*

Long ago, before my grandfather was born, some Eskimo families used to travel from place to place.

One time there was a family of four with an old woman. They lived near Rankin Inlet, N.W.T. The hunting was good for a few years, but not for long. The Uanik family wanted to move to another land called Kanuyalik, where there were lots of caribou. One thing that stopped them was the old woman. She wanted them to leave her. Uanik said he hated to leave her helpless. The old woman asked Uanik if he had forgotten what she had said once. She had said that she would stay behind if they moved away and that she would like to live on the ice that looked like an island.

So Uanik's family, with sorrow in their hearts, left the old woman.

One very clear day the old woman sat on a rock looking at the big ice. She said to herself, "I wish, how I wish, that ice could turn into an island so I could live there."

Two years passed before Uanik came back to the spot where he had left the old woman. The old woman wasn't anywhere on the land. Uanik heard her saying: "Uanik, at last I got my wish, please don't worry anymore." He saw that the ice had turned to marble. "Uanik, my spirit lives on this marble island."

Now, when the people of Rankin Inlet go to the island, they must crawl a few feet in respect of the old woman's spirit. In summer, on a clear day, the island once again looks like an ice island.

Kaivitjvik—Polar Night Festivals
Nuligak

The lifestyle of the Inuit in the western Arctic was very different from that of the spartan Netsiliks on the Boothia. Western communities could be large because men and dogs were supported by whale hunting, and igloos there sometimes had ceilings twelve feet high. Under the circumstances, entertainments such as music and sports were able to flourish, and the long Arctic nights were marked by extensive festivities. In this extract from I, Nuligak *the author recalls the elaborate dramatics which were staged to help pass the time.*

During the period of darkness, the Inuit hardly left their igloos. When the days shortened and the sun was but a little dot on the horizon, the Inuit from the surrounding area would assemble at Kitigariuit for the winter festivities.

Brown bear skins were stuffed to appear alive, and the heads were ingeniously made to produce grunting sounds. White bears were also stuffed, and the paws and claws made to move. As soon as the sun had left the sky the merrymaking began. In those days these holidays took the place of Christmas and New Year festivities. The day was spent watching wrestling matches and eating. As deeper darkness set in, we children would not dare leave the igloo: we were afraid of the bears!

The village had a Chief to organize things and launch the games. This Chief was quite old. When night fell the children squatted on the sleeping platform of the igloo, afraid of the brown and white bears. Suddenly someone would shout, "Aaa!" "Bears" would enter through the katak in the floor, while the Inuit sang amusing songs. Since I was very little, I did not memorize them.

Once the bears were gone, the Inuit would challenge each other in tug-of-war contests; tugging at someone's arm was another way to prove one's strength. Another game was called Orsiktartut, they-make-a-loop. Two ropes were fastened to the vault of the igloo. Someone sitting on the floor would grasp the ends of the ropes and raise himself from the floor. Once raised, he must bring his hands under himself and sit on them. Then he was to return to his first position without touching the floor, and begin all over again. Some would do this five times in a row, while others could not raise themselves from the floor at all. It was not easy. At the end there was a champion!

The Chief would start another game then, a wrestling bout by strength of arms, until one man outdid all the others. In the high jump something was to be touched with the big toe. The Kradjgierk, the igloo used for meetings, had a high ceiling, and the window was in the ceiling, opening on the roof. Some would jump high enough to touch the window with their toe. Others, unable to do this without help, would leap up holding an arrow at arm's length.

Outdoors, we would stand a little sledge on end. The game was to jump over it. One of the winners jumped over a sledge having five transverse bars, that is to say, a height of about seven feet.

On other nights during the festivals, the game organizer would say, "Tonight the Itkrilit, the Indians, will come." He said it so that the children and newcomers would overhear him. That night, with everyone present, the Chief would say, "Sing some more." The song was different, and we children did not know it, for it was a difficult tune. While the singing went on, we heard something strike the house with a loud noise: it was clear that someone was entering the porch. The Chief would say to the stranger, "You have nothing to fear here, come in." And the stranger would leap from the katak to the middle of the floor, and begin to dance. Stopping him in the middle of his dance, the Chief would shout, "Haa!", as if to say "Look at me." Then he would make him talk. "Where do you come from?"

"I come from far away, by a long road. I am cold—I wish to see Inuit. You are glad also to look me over."

The Indian had a knife made of hard wood, and as someone got quite close to him, he drew his knife. He would have struck had not the Chief spoken severely to him. The Indian had strange clothes. His long hair, hiding his face, almost touched the floor as he danced. Whenever the Inuit went to war and killed Indians, they would select those with long hair, tearing it off their heads and scalping them. This they would bring to the most nimble among them, as he was "to be the Indian" during the festivals. That is the reason why this one had such long hair. My grandmother Okonaluk told me that her grandfather, Kinavinak, would keep these dried Indian scalps on hooks on the wall of his igloo. When he needed them to play the Indian he would chew them to soften them. I had asked Grandmother if there was any fat on the scalp. "Not much," she said.

He was a good dancer and the Chief was sorry to stop him. Whenever he jumped it was with great agility and without the least noise. He was always on the alert: That is why he had leapt immediately, knife in hand, to face the one who had approached him from the rear.

The Chief motioned that it was enough. The Indian sprang up to leave when, lo and behold, there in the middle of the floor fell a shower of toys, beads and trinkets, tidbits of caribou fat, and the like. As all these rolled everywhere, the children rushed to gather them up. We had many customs such as these, but I have forgotten some of them.

Now the people wished to see the tunrait, a kind of puppet. The aged people who had made them would work only at night, being careful to avoid being seen by newcomers and children. There was a great variety of these puppets: white bears, brown bears, foxes of all colours, weasels, ducks—and to think that all of them moved as though they were alive! To mystify the children the puppet owners took care not to call these fabricated animals by name. Tunrait was the general name applied to all of them.

On a given night the Chief would launch an appeal to the Inuit to come and show their puppets, calling on this one and that one in particular. The one called upon would shout the name of his tunrar. And there in the opened door appeared the animal—a fox! a bear! We children were frightened!

For instance, the Chief having signed to my grandfather Avilortor to show his tunrar, Avilortor called out in a loud voice. And there a swan hopped over the door sill. It walked into the middle of the floor, stopped, fluttered its wings. It was alive, really alive, as it flapped its wings, looking here and there, stretching and bending its long neck. Besides, this was the month of December, and in the poor light of these sunless days one could have sworn that it was a real swan! At my grandfather's order the swan returned to the katak and disappeared into the passage. Then someone else's turn came. This time a white fox paraded about, going so far as to eat fish scraps from a women's rubbish box—it really seemed to eat!

In those days the Inuit could make marvellous things, many owned puppets like these. To make them I know that whale-bone fibre threads were used, but I do not know how they went about doing it. Before we youngsters could learn from the old, a severe

Nuligak 77

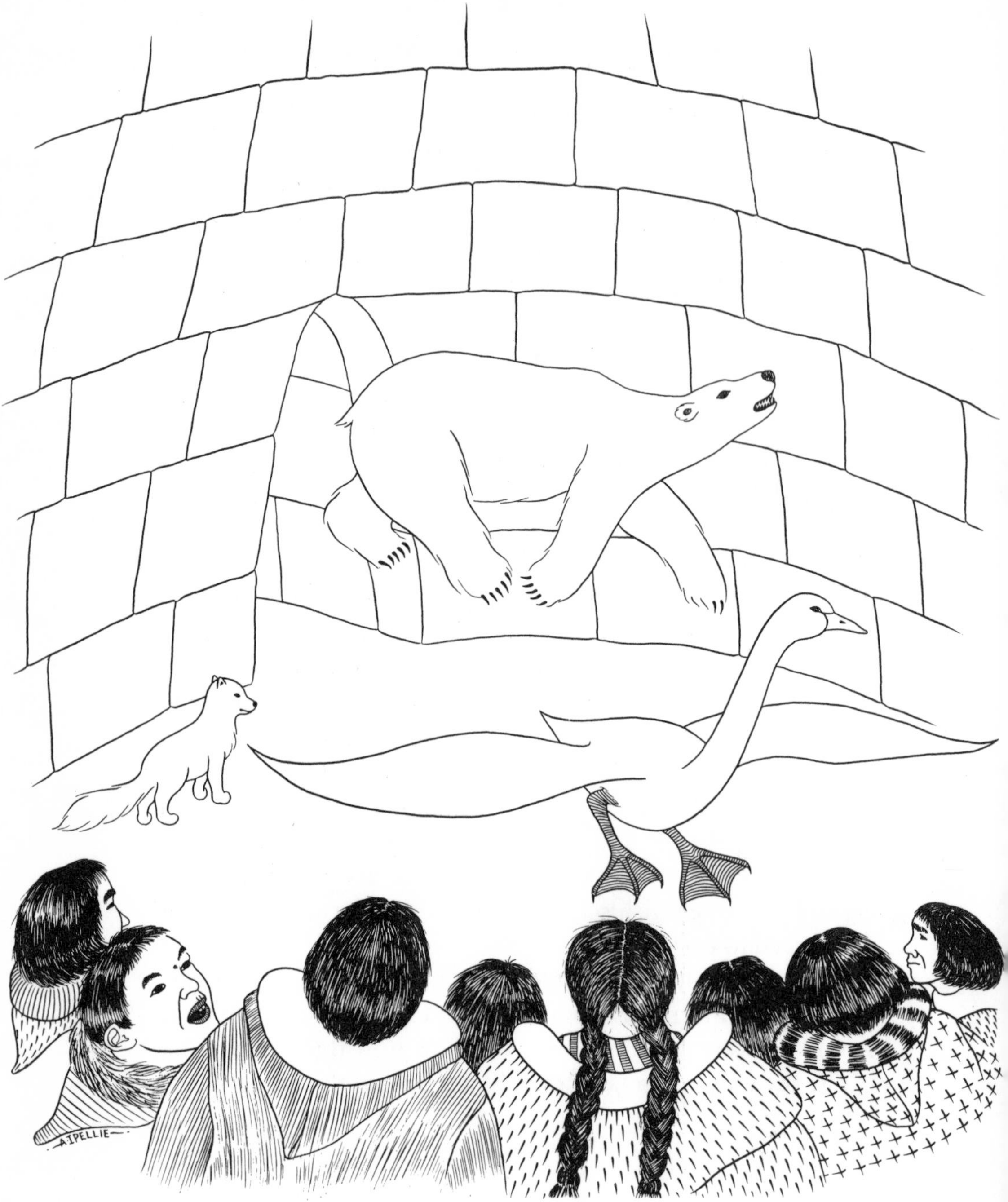
A.IPELLIE

illness carried them away. They were so wary of giving away their secret that it died with them.

During the times of merrymaking that were the night festivals a host of interesting and amazing things was shown. There was such an abundance of meals, games and things to admire that these sunless weeks sped by as if they had been only a few days.

As the sun reappeared and the gatherings were close to an end, we ended our festivals with dart shooting. The dart, there was only one, was balanced by little wings made from a duck's tailfeathers. It flew straight and true. It was carried to each contestant by the one who had made it. The target was a little piece of caribou fat (tunu) thinned out and formed into the shape of a candle, about four inches long and an inch and a half in diameter. It was set in the middle of the floor. The igloo was large and the onlookers many. Men, women and children were all admitted. Someone would set up a prize and another would aim for the target. The greater the stake, the higher the interest rose. Peals of laughter echoed all around. The winner, the one who hit the target, was in turn expected to put up a prize for the next contestant.

Thus ended the last game of the kaivitjvik, the time of dancing and rejoicing which began with the departure of the sun and ended with its return.

Akulak the Shaman
Mrs. Louis Tapatai

Before Christianity was generally accepted by the Inuit, shamans and their magic had a very important place in Inuit society. Mrs. Louis Tapatai had many contacts with shamans; in fact, her father-in-law was a very famous one. In this piece, written for Inuktitut *in 1972, she gives her recollections of Akulak, another famous shaman, who was interviewed by the ethnographer Rasmussen during the Fifth Thule Expedition of 1924, and whose photograph can be found in the reports of that journey.*

Akulak was a small man and was quite thin. He was able to do anything and had no fear of any animal he encountered. He was mighty in the ways of hunting. He was a shaman and wore belts only shamans were allowed to wear. I am not too sure what the belts represented, but when a shaman was travelling to different settlements with a group, all the women would put things on the belt, so that the hunters would have a safe journey and the land would be abundant to them.

The shamans were seen the same way we see doctors today. The shamans were serious men and were hardly seen fooling around.

I will try and explain how Akulak became a Shaman, since the story was told and retold many times. Eqyuayuuk shamanized Akulak. Many of us older people remember who Eqyuayuuk was. He was also a shaman. When they were going to shamanize a person they held drum dances. During the dance the person being shamanized would get shot by the shaman. During a dance Akulak

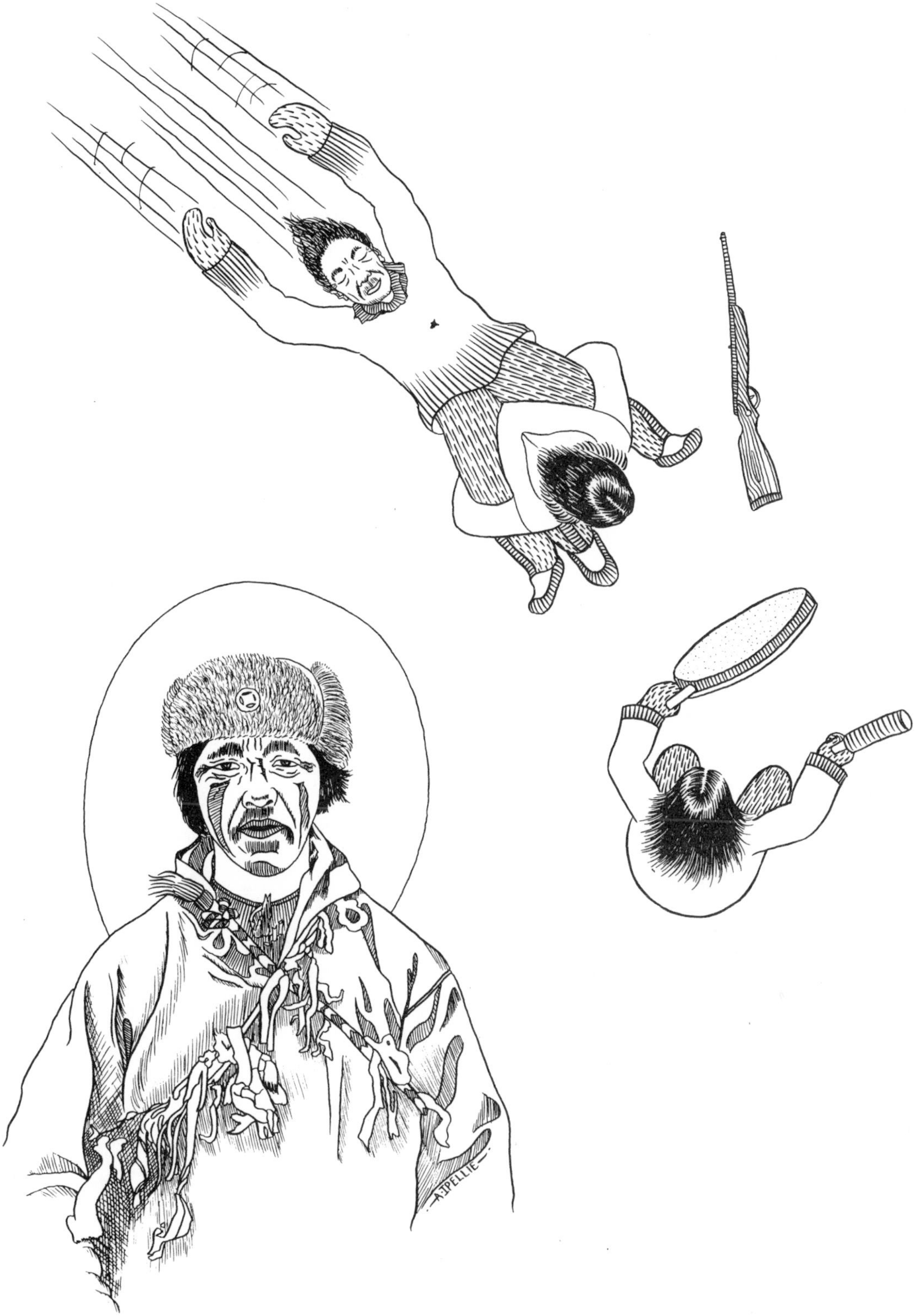
A.IPELLIE

was shot while everyone watched. When Akulak fell to the ground, the pups that were out in the porch started to howl and cry. Akulak was to receive his powers from the pups who were outside. After he died Eqyuayuuk dragged him outside by his two legs. In a short while the two men came back in together as if nothing had happened. Akulak was completely back to normal. No one knows what happened outside the tent, but one shaman went outside the door and two shamans walked back in. I do remember the bullet that was taken out of him after he was shot. The bullet that once killed him was given to him and it was said that if he ever lost the bullet he would automatically die. I have seen the bullet nailed to his wooden case which he took very good care of. Akulak used to cure people even though I never actually saw him practising because I always stayed at home. I used to have problems with my head where every bone would get stiff and impossible to move. He used to do things to me which I still can't understand. My body would get as heavy as a rock and my head was as light as a feather. He would then pull my head which caused much pain, but would cure it everytime. This is all I can say.

Blood-thirsty Enemies
Alexis Pameok Utatnaq

The Inuit have a long-standing satiric tradition. Their famous "song duels" in which two opponents ridiculed each other are things of the past, but the same tongue-in-cheek humour is found in this contemporary verse with its mock-epic introduction. It is taken from the Keewatin Echo *of July 1974. The author, Alexis Utatnaq, is now a well-known folk singer.*

I am appreciative because of the fact that in Canada there is what you call, "Freedom of Speech". And I am most happy to know that many people take that advantage. I, for one, will take this opportunity and write about my ideas.

I am not asking that there be action taken about this but to reinforce to the public about how I feel about what I am about to say.

This may strike you as an inexpectation but it is about enemies. Yes, I or we have an enemy which have been irritating us, agitating us even terrorizing us for many years. Though we have weapons to fight them, it seems they are unconquerable. Their armies are many but weapons are few, like the Japanese suicide squad they are courageous, they are. . . this poem should explain everything:

Our Enemy

Our enemy
They're so many
Our blood they spill
They make us ill

Help us, oh God
From their piercing rod
Our sworn foes
Those mosquitoes

A Sad Case
Laimiki Innuaraq

*This essay, which attempts to capture the nebulous doubts and
fears that torment a man's mind, is probably best described as
stream-of-consciousness; that is, it contains the total range of
unedited thought expressed in a flow of words that resembles the
flow of the mind. It comes from* The Midnight Sun, *an Igloolik
newsletter, for December 1972.*

I am Laimiki Innuaraq and walking straight ahead, I look behind
and change direction. Then I stop and go around and start walking
straight ahead. Then I remember all humans are made the same,
they all have bones. I keep walking straight ahead then I remember
something I can't forget. I feel as though I was in danger. I can't go
to sleep all night because I'm thinking that I'm going to see Jesus.
Then I wonder if there will ever be a tomorrow. Sometimes, when
I'm so tired of thinking, I can't sleep during the night. I know of
two things that can be deeply religious—body and soul in one.
They could separate. How can a person whose soul is departing try
to bring it back, when he had done something which didn't lead to
the path of heaven? I know how to make the way, please tell me
something that I can feel in my heart. Look at me, I'm going the

other way. I'm scared to go the right way because I think I'm not good enough. I think my children are following me. No matter they are mine. Let's try to see the good side of life. You are human and you can think of anything big. It's not visible to your body but is visible in your mind. If it shows on your body it will be noticeable. Nobody knows what's in your mind. When I'm not thinking right I feel a great danger within me, if I don't concentrate on what I have in mind. It makes me feel as though I'm going to be gone in the morning. I have heard that anything can stop working or going. I check on my radio to see if it will stop working, but they still work. I think that if somebody tried to help me through the papers it wouldn't be too good. I'm scared to live right because it makes me think something might happen suddenly. I don't understand my soul—I want very much not to be left behind it. Let me listen to older people if what they are saying is good for me. I hear planes cost a lot to go to other places, but to me they seem to go without any cost once they're gone. Some people may be called tomorrow or some time later or now; they will be called to the destination out of this world, and then they'll be with Jesus. I'm happy and doing something, I've done it and then I regret I've ever done it. Ever since I've been growing up, I've never stopped worrying, even after I got married. I like to pass my time reading our Midnight Sun Newsletter.

Mahaha the Tickler
Marcel Akadlaka

Marcel Akadlaka was a regular contributor to the Keewatin Echo. *His stories were often published alongside the regular news, and sometimes it was difficult to tell fact from fiction. Many of his stories were collected together in the book* How Kabloonat Became and Other Legends, *which is where this one first appeared.*

I have another legend to tell. It is about Mahaha, the tickler. Now these Mahahas kill people, just by tickling them. They have a habit of tickling people.

Once there lived a couple all alone. They were without children. The woman would stay alone while the man was hunting.

While the woman was alone, she went to the porch to her dreadful encounter with a Mahaha. The thing tickled her to death. She lay dead in the porch, still smiling.

The husband was furious to find his wife dead in the porch. From the look on her face, he knew she was tickled to death.

Still furious, he waited in his igloo. When night came around, he went to bed with his clothes on and left the entrance wide open. Suddenly, he heard someone coming in laughing as hard as it could. As he laughed he said, "My father-in-law, ha, ha, ha, ha."

Sure enough the thing started for the man. It climbed up the bed and started to tickle the man. He grabbed it by the ankles and swung it to the floor. Now in the old days when an igloo gets old, the floor becomes ice. As he was swinging the thing to the ice floor, it just kept on laughing as hard as ever. It didn't appear to feel any pain at all.

Thinking he couldn't kill it, he enticed it to go to the water hole with him. At the water hole, he asked it to take a drink. As it bent to take a drink, he pushed it to the hole and drove it under the ice with a scooper. Finally the thing died.

Marcel Akadlaka 87

Medicines from the Past
Martha Angugaatiaq

Martha Angugaatiaq contributed many articles on traditional Inuit culture to the magazine Inummarit. *She wrote about her early life and described in detail many of the tasks a woman had to perform in the old days. This piece was originally called "First Aid Among the Eskimos", and was reprinted in* Inuit Today *in 1975.*

In the past the true Eskimo had all kinds of medicines, which they made themselves. This is what I remember and some of what I heard.

When someone cut himself and was bleeding very much, first they soaked the wound in urine. Then they made a bandage out of fat after removing the oil. A moss called pujuk which looked like cocoa inside was also used. These were used as medicines for cuts. Sometimes animals' gall was used also.

If they cut a vein in one leg and it was bleeding a lot, they tried to stop the bleeding by taping it tight near the cut. Then they would raise the arm or leg.

And for someone who had a boil, they used the skin of lemmings wetting it and fixing it on the boil. When the boil opened they let the pus out.

If there was no lemming skins they used the skin of the arctic hare as a bandage. When the lemming skin was used as a bandage it was called summaqusirsimajuq—waiting for discharge. The brown skin of the lemming was considered better than a gray one.

When someone had infection with pus in it, some Inuit used to open the sore with a small, well sharpened knife to make the pus come out. It was only the braver ones who did these operations.

When someone was drowned the white foam on the mouth was not wiped off, nor did anyone get excited. Sometimes the drowned person would breathe again with the white foam in his mouth.

Ululigarqnaarq
Anonymous

This story has been told and retold so often that its exact meaning has been lost, but even as a story fragment it is cherished. If anything, the embedded meaning and the obscurities add to its impact by stimulating our imagination. This anonymous version was first printed in Inuit Monthly *in 1974.*

There once was a woman who was constantly being mistreated by her husband. Because she did not have any living relatives and her husband would beat her up, she would often go outdoors and cry her eyes out. In those days, Inuit believed that their dead relatives would go up into another world. When the night fell, she would go outside and cry, remembering her dead relatives. She would look up to the sky at the moon and cry out, "Come and get me! Come and get me!"

One night while she was crying, she heard a sound similar to the howl of the wind. When she looked around, she saw a dog team approaching from the sky. When the dog team arrived, she was told to get on the sleigh facing backwards. She was also told to cover her face inside her parka top. He did not want her looking around because the moon was shining and everything was bright. She followed his instructions and covered her face and got on the sleigh facing backwards on her stomach. "We will be travelling at a very high speed and if you try and look, you might fall off, so do not try and see where we are going. Stay put the way you are now and only if I tell you to move or look, then you may," said the man. When they started to take off, the man called out to all of his dogs by name.

When they had taken off, the wind was strong against her for they were travelling at a very high speed. She started to get curious as to which route she was travelling, and started to sneak a tiny peek through the fur of her parka top. "Ah ah ah" was the warning of the driver of the dog team. One of her mittens flew off even before she had a chance to take a peek.

She did not dare take any more chance after that. Finally, she felt that they had landed. The driver called out to his dogs again by their names and gave his passenger permission to get up. There before her were several igloos.

She was then directed to enter what seemed to be the biggest igloo. "When you enter, go sit down in the centre of the bed," said the man. When she entered, she sat down where she was told.

When she looked around, she noticed that they were all women sitting with their knees tucked inside their stomachs. The eldest of them spoke to her, "Because I'm gigglish, I'm now in my condition." Then she saw that the old lady did not have any internal organs. She had no intestines and when she laughed, her laugh was hollow and sounded as if it was from great distance. "Ululigarqnaarq will be coming shortly. She will act foolish and try and make you laugh. If you do laugh then you too will turn out like me.

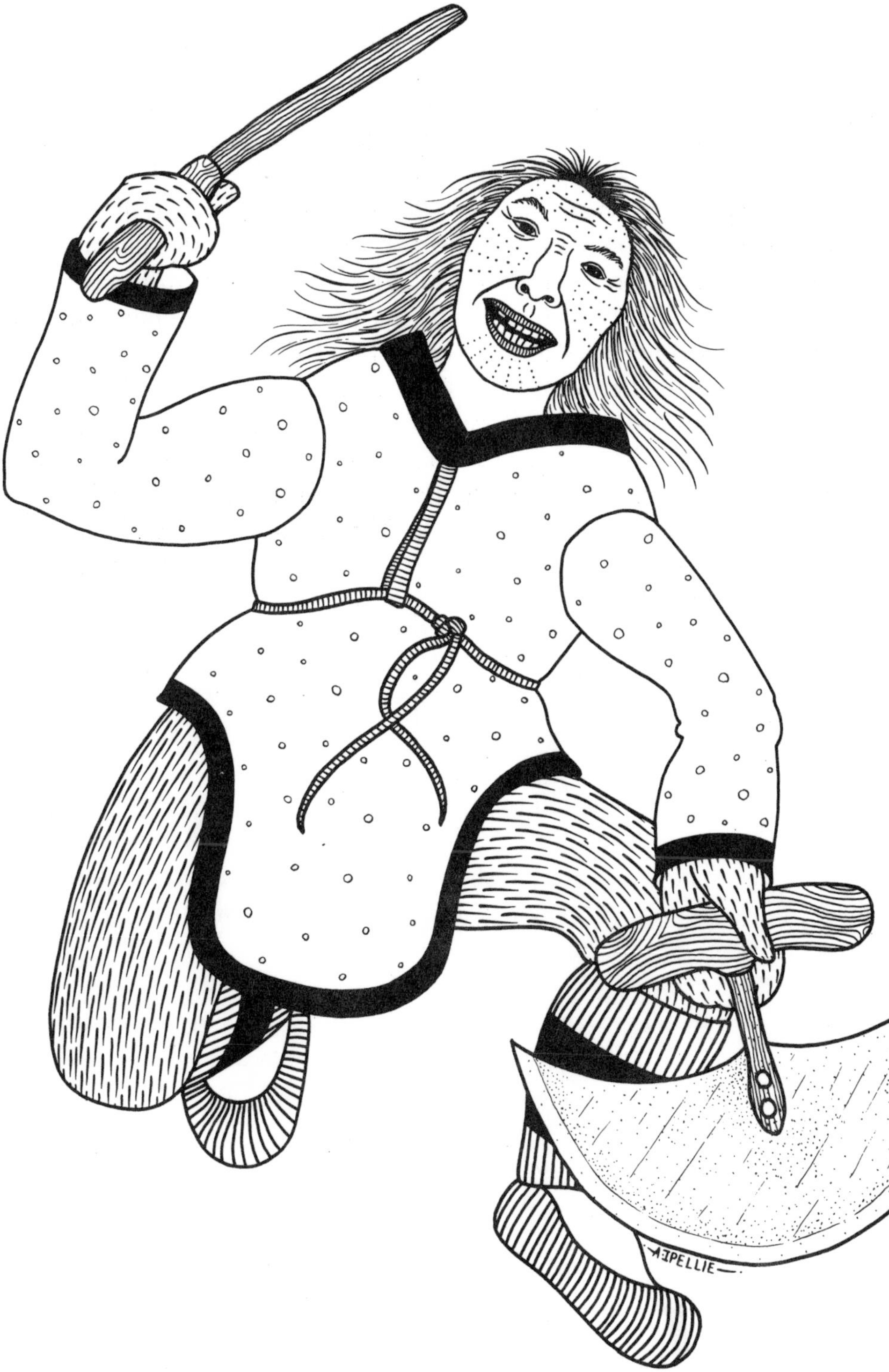
A. IPELLIE

If you begin to feel gigglish, make your hand in the image of a polar bear and put it between your legs from underneath, then blow on it. She'll do everything to make you laugh!" Even before she completed the sentence, in came Ululigarqnaarq. She was an old lady with tattoos on her face. She held in her hand a huge ulu and knife sharpener. She started to swing her huge ulu as if it was a drum while beating it with the knife sharpener. She tilted her head up and closed her eyes and danced around right in front of the visitor, swinging her head from side to side. She danced and sang about her tattoos while doing everything to make the visitor laugh.

When the visitor started to feel gigglish, she made her hand in the image of a polar bear, put her hand underneath her legs and in between her legs, then blew on it. When she did that, Ululigarqnaarq cried out something referring to blubber that the polar bear have and left.

Morning Mood
Mary Panegoosho

"Morning Mood" is probably one of the best known contemporary Inuit poems, and no collection of Eskimo writing would be complete without it. Mary Panegoosho's poem evokes a spirit which is found in the "matchbox" houses of the settlements or the tents and igloos of the camps, a spirit which is thoroughly Inuit.

I wake with morning yawning in my mouth,
With laughter, see steaming a tea kettle spout.
I wake with hunger in my belly
And I lie still, so beautiful it is, it leaves me dazed,
The timelessness of the light.

Grandma cares for me, and our family needs nothing more.
They share each other for pleasure
As mother knows, who learns of happiness
From her own actions
They did not even try to be beautiful, only true,
But beauty is here, it is a custom.

This place of unbroken joy,
Giving out its light today—only today—not tomorrow.

The Half-Fish
Taivitialuk Alaasuaq

The female sea spirit, Sedna as she is sometimes called, is the most powerful and dangerous of the ancient Inuit spirits. All the animals of the land and sea originate with her, and if she is angered, starvation will surely follow. This story, by a Povungnituk carver, attempts to reconcile the old beliefs with the technology brought North by the white traders.

A man was out hunting on foot looking for driftwood along the shore. Over in the distance, while still far off, he saw a creature half-fish and half-human on the shore waving to him. As it kept waving, he went over to it. And so when he arrived,

"Don't come close. Don't come close; just stay nearby," said the half-fish.

"Then how can I get you into the water without touching you?" said the man.

"You are looking for wood. Find some wood and try to push me out into the water. If you push me out, I will reward you," it said.

So then, looking for wood, he got some to try to push it out into the water. As it was really stuck fast in the rocks and as the half-fish was very heavy, he worked a long time. When at last he pushed it out in the water, the half-fish said to him,

"At dawn I will place here a gramophone, a gun, and a sewing machine."

And so the half-fish went off, far away out there in the water. The man simply went home. Then when dawn came, the man returned to the shore to the spot where he had pushed the creature out to sea. And there on the shore the half-fish had put a gramophone, a gun, and a sewing machine. But it was nowhere to be seen. The gramophone, the sewing machine, and the gun, just these were found. And so all the white men are learning [to do as the half-fish did] we people are thinking. That's the way the story goes; I stop because it's finished.

Taivitialuk Alaasuaq 95

Nipikti the Old Man Carver
Alootook Ipellie

The Inuit Co-operative Federations play an important part in life in the North. In some settlements in the North people rely on them for everything from water delivery and garbage disposal to the buying of carving for resale in the South. This story by Ipellie, which first appeared in Nunatsiaq News, *gives some idea of how ritualized buying day at the Co-op has become for many old Inuit carvers.*

Nipikti was now an old man and took three times as long as any young Inuk to get from one point to another. Almost every week, he would get up from his small carving studio at home and start walking out to the Co-op where he sold at least a half a dozen carvings he had finished during the week. He hung the bag of carvings over his shoulder and started out the door, his walking stick leading the way for him.

"This is the day I will get the upper hand of the deal with the Co-op manager. I have no doubt that he will fall in love with the carving I finished today," he said as he closed the door behind himself.

On the way to the Co-op, Nipikti would stop several times to rest his tired old legs by sitting on the same rocks he had sat on for the last twenty years or so.

"Ahhh! Hi, Ojagajaak, it feels good to rest on you," he would say to the first rock, as if the rock was an old friend of his. "These legs of mine are a little weaker than last week, so I will have to sit on you for an extra five minutes if you do not mind."

There he sat to rest on Ojagajaak and looked across the land where he had lived as a young man. That is the place where he had hunted the good animals of the land. That is where he had taken care of his wife and family when they were growing up. "Those were good times of the past," he thought, "times when carvings like these were toys and tokens to us Inuit."

He got up slowly and continued on to the Co-op where he would get the money to support his family. The Co-op was still quite far away.

"If I had my way, I would prefer to carve the stones and ivory to make toys for my children, and hunt the animals like I used to. I wasn't such a bad hunter in those days," Nipikti said to himself.

"I never thought I would be living off the very carvings I used to make only to keep my children happy."

Nipikti finally came to the rock where he sat to rest the second time along the way to the Co-op and said, "How are you today Ojagakaluk? I have come again to rest on you. I am an old man now, you know."

He sat on Ojagakaluk and took enough rest there to make it to the next rock. "I shall see you again on my way back. Just make sure the bulldozer doesn't push you under before then," Nipikti shouted back to the second rock as he slowly started walking on.

When he came to the third rock, he sat down and said, "You know, Ojagakutaaq, you are probably the most comfortable rock I have ever sat on in my life. I must say I will certainly miss you the day they remove you from this spot to make way for the new road. You have been a good rock to me and I must thank you in case they start building the road while I am at the Co-op."

He then got up to walk the last leg of the trip to the local Co-op and said to himself that it was time to think about how much he would persuade the Co-op manager to pay him for his carvings. Especially for the good one he finished earlier that day.

"I should be able to sell the good carving for $150 easily," he said. "I'm sure there isn't any other carving this week that was done any better than this one."

When he got to the Co-op, Nipikti took the six carvings out of the bag and laid them on the desk for the manager to look at.

The manager picked up the carvings one by one and looked them over carefully. When he came to the carving Nipikti had done that day, he immediately offered Nipikti $120 for it.

Nipikti stood leaning on his walking stick and counted on $150 as planned. Nipikti knew by experience that the carving was worth that much or even more. "$150," he said.

The manager looked up at Nipikti's face, then picked up the carving in question and mused over the fine detail of the work Nipikti had done. "Okay," he finally said, "I'll give you $130 for it."

Nipikti looked at the manager's face and thought about the last offer for $130. "If you think you are going to play games with me, you might as well be prepared to do it for the rest of the day. I am not going to play that long," he said in Inuktitut.

The manager clearly understood that Nipikti was not about to change his original asking price of $150. He knew that the price was right for the carving. But he decided to try once more to buy the carving for less than that. "140," he said.

Nipikti just stood there and cleared his throat, then said for the last time, "150." And with that, he tapped the top of the desk with his right hand. It was a sign that he meant business.

At that moment, the manager decided to give up trying to persuade the old carver to say yes to what he wanted and agreed to pay the $150 he was asking for.

Nipikti had won the battle this time around. He took the money for the carvings he'd brought in and went out the door to begin his journey back home with his walking stick in hand and money in his pocket to support the family for the next few weeks. He looked across the land and saw that the three rocks where he sat to rest each week were still there. No one had started to build the road yet. And he just smiled and said to himself that it was good.

"I had better make sure that they do not bulldoze my rocks away. The way I see it, I am sure to win my case over that too," he said for the last time, and he slowly moved on toward home where he would start the next carving.

Nipikti the old man carver lives on.

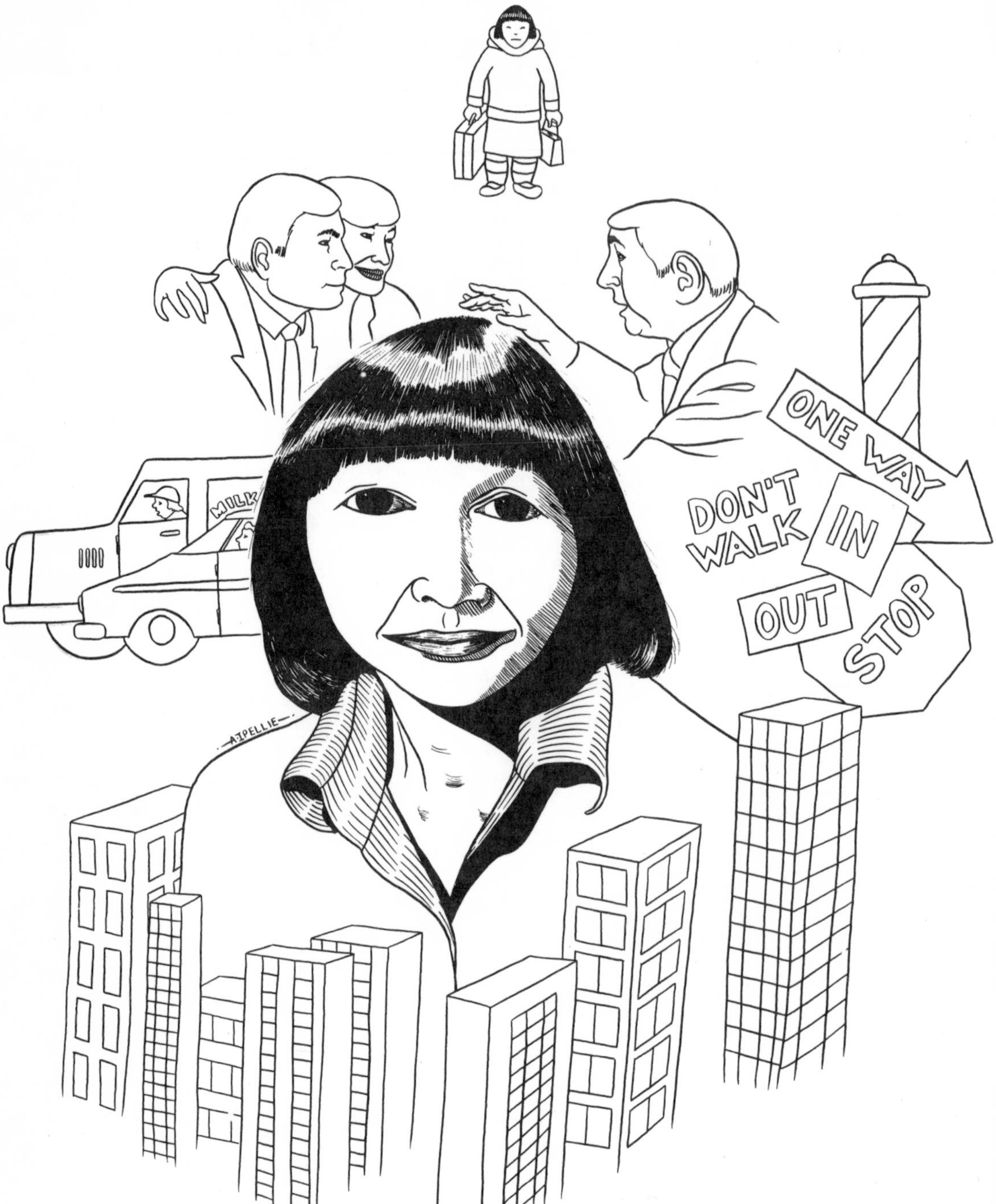

MILK
ONE WAY
DON'T WALK
IN
OUT
STOP
A.I.PELLIE

Survival in the South
Minnie Aodla Freeman

Minnie Freeman was born on Cape Hope Island in the James Bay. She came South to work as a translator for the government when she was twenty years old, and never forgot those first dreadful months in Ottawa. This play, Survival in the South, *was written when she was living in Newfoundland. It was produced for the Dominion Drama Festival in 1971, was later staged in Ottawa, and was adapted as a radio play for the CBC. A fuller treatment of Minnie's introduction to the South can be found in her book,* Life Among the Qallunaat, *published in 1978.*

Dramatis Personae

NARRATOR, an Eskimo woman
MINNIE AODLA, a young translator on her first visit to the south
MR. GORDON, CHIEF, A WOMAN — Employees of the Department of Indian Affairs
MATRON, superintendent of the women's residence
JANE, Minnie's roommate at the residence
POLICEMAN
RECEPTIONIST at a hairdressing salon

Prologue

NARRATOR

There is no doubt that much has been written about Eskimo people. There is also no doubt that there is little known about their basic culture.

Traditionally Eskimos were nomadic; survival at every season depended on their hunting success. Such was the manner of my early life. My parents belonged to a group that moved around Hudson Bay and James Bay region. According to Qallunaat history books, Henry Hudson had discovered Hudson and James Bay. To me, he visited and saw the region, but my ancestors found it long before him.

My grandfather was the leader of seven families. He had led these people in the late 1800s up to 1940s from the Belcher Islands along the coast of Hudson Bay and James Bay, until he found Cape Hope Island which he named after himself, "Weetaltuk Island". There he settled the seven families. To lead people in our culture one has to have wisdom concerning human nature, knowledge of the weather, and the ability to predict where and when the hunting will be most successful. No moves are made till the leader says so. Though he led the group it does not mean he made every choice for every individual. Family heads still had to lead their own families in matters such as bringing up children. In my culture I was brought up to listen and obey my elders, not to ask but to follow, and not to give advice until I have reached that stage where I am considered to have gained wisdom. Not until I am on my own, such as after marriage, was I allowed to choose my clothing and what I wanted to do. As long as I was with my guardians I had no choice but to take what was given to me.

I came South before I was ever considered in my culture "to be on my own". On arrival in the south, I suddenly found myself in a totally new world, and had to start learning from the beginning once again how to survive each day.

But how does one live in a totally different world and yet survive? My parents always told me, when not knowing what to do, and consequently afraid, I should always put on my best front—that is, smile, use my sense of humour and above all remain curious and alert so as to take every advantage of opportunities to learn new things. Moreover, as I grew older...

...I was taught never to react outwardly to exasperation.
(Sound: train—loud then fade)
I alight from the train on my arrival in the South for the first time.
(Train enters, brakes, changes into people)
So many gates. Which one should I use?... How are people going to know I have arrived? What shall I do?...I wish I was home and see a familiar face...so many people, moving like maggots on rotten meat.
(All stop—continue)
How long am I going to stand here? Oh! the ground is hard on my feet. I suppose I am not allowed to take my shoes off? It is so hot!
MR. GORDON

Miss Aodala? *(All stop)* My name is Gordon. Did you have a good trip? I'll look after your luggage, you will live in a very nice place. You will work with some very nice people, you will have a very nice time. Oh, you have the baggage tickets? Simply follow me.
(All start)
NARRATOR

So many people! doing so many different things...walking...

Minnie Aodla Freeman 103

talking...eating...drinking...reading and someone talking in a cupboard!...Oh. I am so hot!, my feet ache...everything is going so fast...

MR. GORDON

Now I'll drive you where you live...you'll like it there, there are over 300 girls. You'll eat there...you'll meet the matron there... you'll get everything you want there...bla bla bla bla...

NARRATOR

I still have to travel?...300 girls? All I want right now is a tent to myself to have a good cry and see my parents.

(Cue for green traffic lights, traffic goes mad)

(Shouting) How does he know which car to take? My first car ride...oh he's going to hit another one...look in front of me... so many cars...where are they going?...

(Cue for red light, traffic stops)

Why have we stopped?

(Cue for green light, traffic starts)

Oh, so many things to see, so many stores...so many people walking fast and looking so sad...look at the height of that house.

(Traffic exits)

MR. GORDON

Here we are, only a short trip, I'll take your luggage...

NARRATOR

He is so concerned about my luggage.

MR. GORDON

Ah, matron. *(Minnie sits)* Eskimo! Never been South before, she'll need extra help, you'll have to show her round, explain the rules, etc. *(They both look at her)* Must be tired, been on the train two days—o.k.?—I'll see her in the office tomorrow, make sure she gets there, 8:30 sharp. See ya tomorrow Miss Aodala—Gee, look at the time, I gotta fly—phew—*(Exits)*

104   *Minnie Aodla Freeman*

MATRON

Miss Aodolah. I am the matron here. Come this way and I'll show you to your room. You will have a roommate but you won't meet her yet as she is still working...Oh, here is the book of house rules—follow me...

NARRATOR

Oh my feet ache—it is so hot.

MATRON

This is your room...here is your locker...the combination is 141256—141256—got that? Your bed will be changed once a week, meals are from 6:30 to 7:30 a.m., 11:30 to 12:30 noon and 5:30 to 6:30 p.m. Make sure you're not late for meals, you pay for your room at the end of each month. Here is your key...just come any time you are having problems, and don't forget to study the house rules.

(Exit)

NARRATOR

So many things I mustn't forget, so many things I must remember: lock combination, change the bed, meal hours, paying my room, I wonder if the girl I room with has to do the same? I will just follow her...she will soon come...Oh I am afraid, I wish to go home and see someone I know and talk to someone oh—someone is coming.

JANE

Hi! *(Loud)*

MINNIE

(No answer)

JANE

My name Jane...you...Eskimo?!

MINNIE

Yes.

Minnie Aodla Freeman   105

JANE
Really! Uh...where do Eskimos come from?
MINNIE
From the Arctic.
JANE
Arctic, eh—uh—I learned in Geography that Eskimos rub noses—live in snow houses, and—eat raw meat—Did you do all that?
NARRATOR
This girl has no self control.
MINNIE
Yes!
JANE
Really?
(Pause)
Are you shy? You don't say much. I guess you're shy.
NARRATOR
True, no sense of control.
JANE
Say, what's your name? What'll we call you?
MINNIE
Minnie—Minnie Aodla.
JANE
Gee, that's cute, my name's Jane.
(Pause)
MINNIE
Can I unpack my things?
JANE
Sure! I'll help. Oh, that's real cute—oh—yeah—heh—that's nice—aha—oh yeah. (She hangs them up) But, is that all? But...where are your clothes?
MINNIE
There.

JANE
I mean your own . . . *personal* . . . clothes.

MINNIE
They are mine.

JANE
No, your clothes where you come from, you know, *SKINS!*
(Pause)

NARRATOR
This girl is out of control.

JANE
Sorry. I didn't mean to pry into your affairs, I really expected skins.

NARRATOR
I do wish not to be so shy. I would take time to inform her about skin clothing.

JANE
Well, I guess it's bed-time. Are you working tomorrow?

MINNIE
Yes.

JANE
Where? With who?

MINNIE
Department of Northern Affairs.

JANE
Doing what?

MINNIE
Translating.

JANE
From your language to ours?

MINNIE
I guess. I will know better tomorrow.

JANE
Well, time to turn in—

(She begins to undress, turns away from Minnie, lights fade)
Good night Minnie.
MINNIE
Good night Jane.
(Sound of breakfast, etc., all cast enters for breakfast, eat on their feet and go, leaving Minnie stranded)
WOMAN
Oh. I can't remember your name. Matron did tell me yesterday . . . er—are you the Eskimo?
NARRATOR
She is out of control too.
WOMAN
Fine! I'll take you to the office, simply follow me.
(They walk to the street crossing, then stop is the cue for the red traffic lights, enter traffic, rush by and then exit. Exit is cue for green traffic lights, Minnie follows woman)
NARRATOR
Nothing seems to bother her. There is so much to see and yet she doesn't seem to notice anything. She seems to have only one thing in her mind, to get to her destination . . . my feet ache . . . how far yet to go? Now, what are we waiting for? A bell?
(All rush into the elevator which ascends)
I'm squashed—I can't breathe—we go upwards—want air—oh.
(Elevator arrives—crowd disperse)
CHIEF
Ah, here we are, glad to meet you again Miss Aodala . . . Are you ready to work for me?
NARRATOR
He says my name so ugly. Oh I feel shy. What will happen to me now? He looks gentle, but I'm still afraid.

CHIEF

I will have to ask you a few questions just so we have something on our files.

(Pause)

If you prefer I can wait till some other time.

(Freeze)

NARRATOR

He is gentle. . . How I wish to tell him that I am afraid. . . that I am not used to what I have gone through for the last twenty-four hours. . . that I have seen so much that never entered my mind that they exist. . . that my feet ache. . . that I have left my family and friends. . . have endured my first long train ride to a train station. . . to a car ride. . . to strange living quarters with strange rules for living. . . and walked for the first time on a stone path. . . and for the first time gone up in a strange machine so that my breathing can't seem to take the air outside. . . Wish this lump in my throat would go away. . . don't think I can hold those tears anymore. . . I need to cry. . .

CHIEF

What's wrong? Did I offend you?. . . I guess you're tired?. . . You have to answer me so I can help you. Are you not happy where you're living? Did anything happen yesterday? I know—you have a good cry and I'll get you some coffee. *(He goes for some)*

(Returning with coffee) Here we are—I'll show you where your desk is and leave you some letters to translate. I'd like to see them when you're finished because I have to know how well you do, maybe you'll feel better tomorrow. You can go home at lunch hour, take the afternoon off.

(He motions to secretary, she follows chief, office stops to look at Minnie, then all continue—slow fade and then back on lunch

bell—all rush for elevator to descend) (Bell)

NARRATOR

(in elevator) How will I get back home? If I get lost I must ask a policeman. He wears a blue uniform.

(People rush out)

I'll just follow those people into the street, I won't pay attention to the names of the streets, I will only look at the signs and colours and shapes. That's how I will remember the way.

(Exits then returns to street noises)

MINNIE

Oh!

(Lights change to red and traffic bursts in and then out, lights turn green, Minnie moves on)

NARRATOR

I am very alone... so many tall buildings, I can't see how far the sun has dropped... Ah, there is a policeman. I will ask him where I live.

(She approaches policeman)

MINNIE

Can you please tell me where Sussen Street is?

POLICEMAN

Speak up ma'am. Where was it?

MINNIE

Please, where is Sussen Street?

POLICEMAN

Sussen? That way, ten blocks.

NARRATOR

Ten blocks. Aukatalangani! My feet are aching, I am so hot, I have to find my way home. I vow to myself tomorrow I will look at my route better. Tomorrow? What is tomorrow? Today is four, the next is five, so tomorrow is number five.

Ah! Today, I don't care if I'm lost all day . . . I'm going to see many things . . . I'll just walk and walk. Look at the shops, tall buildings, I will look at anything I can see.

(Enter revolving door)

Oh! What is that?

(She attempts to enter store but doesn't make it; then the hairdresser's shop materializes)

I will go in here and see what they do. *(Bell)*

(Enters shop)

RECEPTIONIST

Yes. You have an appointment? What is your name? Did you want a wash and set—the works? *(Pause)* Do you speak English?

MINNIE

Yes.

RECEPTIONIST

Did you make an appointment to have your hair done?

MINNIE

No.

RECEPTIONIST

Well, I guess we can fit you in. What is it you want done?

(No answer)

How would you like it done?

MINNIE

What do you do here?

RECEPTIONIST

Curled, cut or just dried?

MINNIE

Everything!

RECEPTIONIST

You don't want it cut, it's such beautiful hair, is it natural, do you dye it? It's so black.

MINNIE
Everything!
RECEPTIONIST
O.K. Marvin! One for the works!
(*Lights red for hair cutting ritual*)
(*They exit leaving Minnie with new hair do*)
MINNIE
My head feels nice and cool, now I'm ready to work.
(*Change to boardroom scene*)
CHIEF
Now, this meeting is called to discuss our future programmes, and top of the list is—er—Miss Aodala—er—we are planning to begin training some of our people from here in the South to enable them to survive in the North. The title of this programme I name called—er—"How to survive in the North" (*general reaction*). Now, Miss er Aodala—if you have any suggestions for use—we in this group will be very pleased to consider them.
(*Fade to half and focus on Minnie*)
NARRATOR
They ask me how to survive, they don't tell me how to survive in the South . . . I am not worthy for these people . . . I am nothing to them; it does not matter whether I survive or not in their country; I am nothing to them, therefore, I have to help them in how to survive in my land—ugh, it's hot in this place . . .
(*Fade to end*)

A Song
Ivaluardjuk

"For many years the people of Igloolik have sung songs and told stories. This is an old song that Ivaluardjuk, Uyarak's uncle, sang many years ago." This is how the following song was introduced when it was printed in The Midnight Sun Newsletter *ten years ago. It was recorded on paper by Knud Rasmussen during The Fifth Thule Expedition about fifty years ago.*

Cold and mosquitoes,
These two pests
Come never together.
I lay myself down on the ice,
Lay myself down on the snow and ice,
Till my teeth fall chattering.
It is I.
Aja—aja—aja.

Memories are they,
From those days,
From those days,
Mosquitoes swarming
From those days,
The cold is bitter,
The mind grows dizzy
As I stretch my limbs
Upon the ice.
It is I.
Aja—aja—aja.

Ai! but songs
Call for strength
And I seek after words,
I, aja—aja—aja.

Ai! I seek and spy
Something to sing of,
The caribou with the spreading antlers!

And strongly I threw
The spear with my throwing stick
And the weapon fixed the bull
In the hollow of the groin
And it quivered with the wound
Till it dropped
And was still.

Ai! but songs
Call for strength,
And I seek after words.
It is I,
Aja—aja—aia—haja—haja.

I Make My Living by Carving
Marius Kayotak

In the book We Don't Live in Snow Houses Now, *the residents of the community of Arctic Bay talk about their past, the changes they have seen, and their present lives. A big part of life today in Arctic Bay is concerned with the production of Eskimo soapstone carving. In this section, taken from an interview with a young carver, it becomes obvious how seriously the artists take their work.*

I was born in Akkunik, close to Igloolik, and I lived with my grandparents. We used to live in camp until I started going to school, first in Chesterfield Inlet, then in Churchill and Winnipeg. In Chesterfield we were taught by nuns; I was really scared of them.

I don't remember when people began to carve. I think some of them started when the co-op was started in Igloolik by Father Fournier, in about 1962. I think I remember that it made fifty dollars the first year. It was the next year that I did my first carving, some sort of a man and a polar bear as usual. I was about sixteen and I was interested in it. The prices were very low at that time—I think I got seventeen dollars for my first carving. I was very pleased, but I had worked at that carving nearly every night for a month. I had very poor tools, just a file and an axe to chip it.

I forgot about carving, just left it, for about three years. Then I started again, doing little carvings. Since everybody liked them, I continued and they kept getting bigger. In 1969 I was a carpenter's apprentice in Frobisher Bay and I did some carving for a man there;

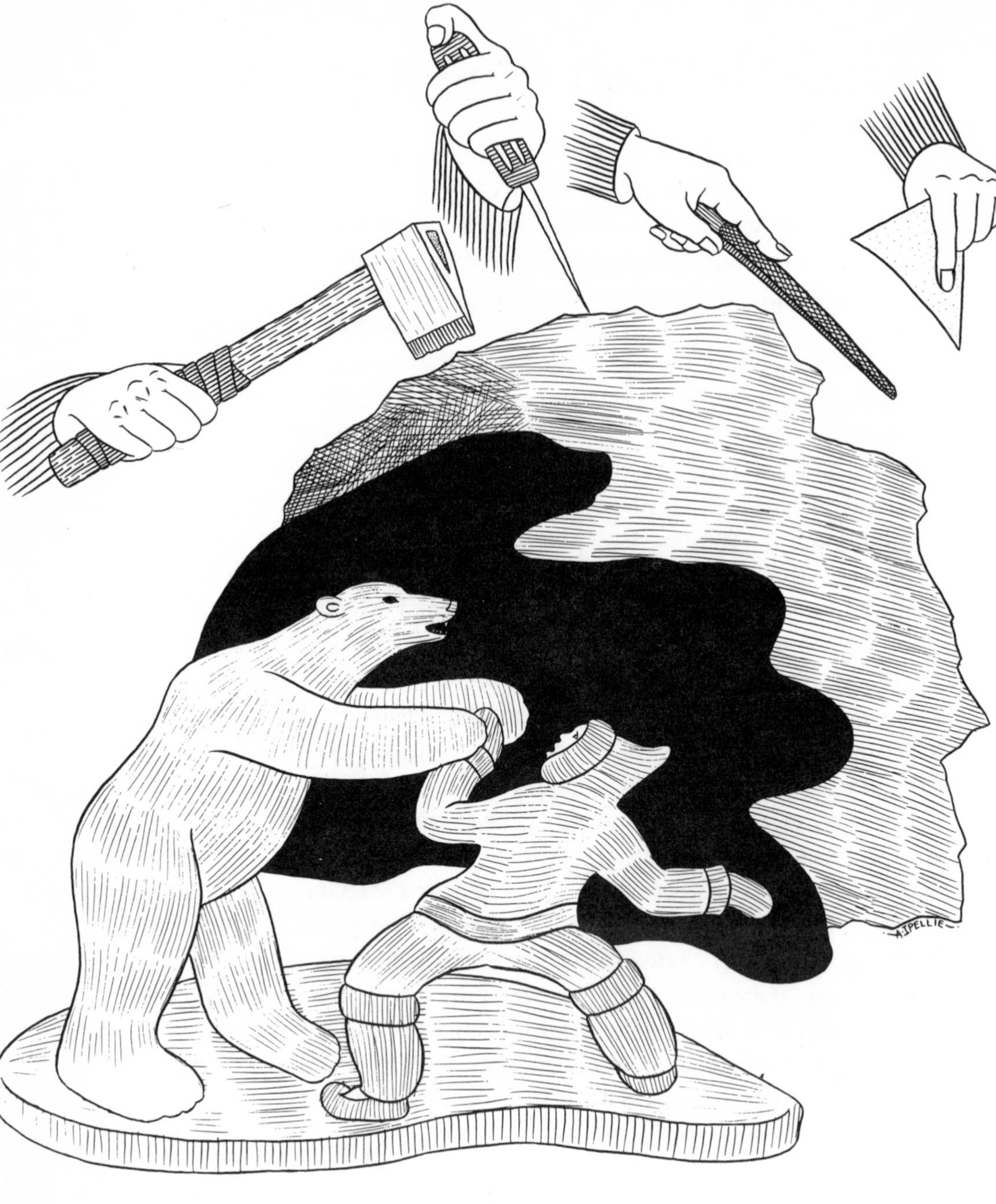
AIPELLIE

I just used to practice, you know, for little gifts, nothing very much. Then this man found out that I carved. I quit my job and started carving and we were doing all right. This man used to buy small carvings and price them the same as the big ones. He sent my large carvings down south. I don't know where any of my carvings are, but I remember most of them.

Creating a carving from a piece of soapstone is very, very interesting to me. I take a look at a piece of rock that I've just found; start working on it; it starts coming out; and, after a while, it finishes. I like to do several figures in one piece—that's very interesting to me and it's quite hard to do the inside. I really like that. I don't know how many carvings I've made of a polar bear and a man from one piece, but they always come out. I just start chipping off the stone. Sometimes I don't know where I'm going to put an arm or the legs, because I haven't figured it out first, but it always comes out. To me, a figure of a man and a polar bear, and maybe a couple of dogs, in one piece of rock is the hardest thing I can carve. After you've been doing that sort of carving, you can make one piece of carving in action or just in a simple form. You can make a carving of a man in less than five hours and get a good price for it. The faster I go, the more excited I get.

To do a polar bear walking is very easy for me, so I like to do combination carvings because they are more difficult. I never make them the same.

I don't use power tools, except to do a hand that is going to hold something. Then I drill. I like to make [a carving] by hand; if I use power tools it's more somebody else's than mine. I use a sharpened screwdriver to chip away the insides. If I have a piece of stone that I want to break at a certain angle I use an axe, give it about two chops, and cut it. You have to know what you're doing

Marius Kayotak 117

with the stone—where the grains and cracks are. If you do it wrong, one chop could ruin everything. When I started carving I used to break a lot of pieces, but not any more. Now I know the stone 98% better!

When I was in Frobisher Bay, I bought a carving from their co-op. After I paid for it, they asked me why I had bought it when I could do it myself. I told them I like anybody else's carvings. I never really like my own. Sometimes my mind is completely out of focus, you know, and I can't carve, so I'll ask the person who wants a carving what he would like. He usually says, "Do what you like and I'll like it." That's really hard.

Maybe the reason that people like my carvings is that I don't make them in simple form. Most of them are motion figures; if you turn the piece around or even upside down, it seems to have movement in it. That's why people buy them.

This summer (after moving from Igloolik to Arctic Bay), I was looking for the area up there where they find the grey and red soapstone. The people here gave me directions, but I couldn't find it even though I went twice to look. So I told my grandmother that I was going to look for a piece of soapstone of my own, and in forty-five minutes time I had been for a walk and found a good piece. From that stone I'm going to make some carvings, and I hope people will like it. There's not much of the green stone left, and the grey stone is getting very thin and the pieces aren't very big. I don't mean to do big carvings, but I want to be free to do any figure I want. With this white stone that I've found I am, because the stone is all loose—at the top there are smaller pieces and as you go down further, the pieces get bigger. I've never seen that kind of stone before. Some of it is very hard, as hard as the green stone, and some of it has colours in it. It looks a little bit like marble, but it's not. I've seen a geologist and he said it wasn't marble. For me, the harder the stone the easier it is to carve because you can chip it off better. You can't chip soft stone, your axe just bounces.

I found that stone and I'm going to do fifty carvings from it. For about two years I've been interested in doing a lot of carvings and selling them all at once—maybe having some kind of show. I've even ordered some shelves from Simpson's Sears so I can have them in my house until I have finished and can sell them all together. I want to finish my carvings around September, six or seven months from now, but in order to do that I'm going to have to have some money—mainly for food. Now that I've started, I don't want to stop. If I need money, I might not sell them. I might go to Strathcona Sound for a couple of months or so, make some money, and then start my carvings again. But that's going to take a long time and I might want to stay there rather than do my carvings. I'm going to finish them before September though.

[Once I've finished those fifty carvings], I'll go farther south, Los Angeles or something. I'll have better tools by then. One day I would like to make a really big carving—about my size, anyway. I wouldn't mind doing a man and a polar bear, life size, but where would I get the stone? I'd like to do a carving like that even if it wouldn't sell.

In the summertime, I always enjoy looking for rocks. I carry a file or a knife, and if I see something I try to chip it; if I can carry it I take it home. When we were working at the mine, it was a messy job. I'd rather be looking for stone on the surface. One of the surveyors at the mine told me that I should take up geology. I told him that I wasn't in a position to because my grade was too low. He said it would be easier to find the stone I want. I told him that I can always find the stone I want, that I've found some already. I don't have to take up geology just to find soapstone. As a matter of fact, I believe I'm going to find something in a couple of weeks time, something that has fallen from one of the stars. We went out last night to get our skidoos, about one o'clock, and we saw a falling star land right on the mountain side. When it landed you could even see the smoke coming out of the snow. I'm pretty sure I can find some pieces. It actually landed where we could see it, not very far from here. It was very bright, a blueish colour—when I looked away I couldn't see anything. I've seen falling stars before (I don't even know whether they landed or not), but when I saw this one land, I said to myself: I'm going to go and find it.

I like drafting. When I was in vocational school we did some drafting, carpentry, electrical work, mechanics and so on, three months of each subject. After I finished, I went to Winnipeg to learn carpentry. I was a carpenter's apprentice in Frobisher at the time I began to make my living by carving. When I was young we used to live in a little matchbox house, and in the winter it was very cold. When I got into carpentry and drafting, I used to do a lot of drawings, designing things like the corners, the floor plans and construction of the houses. I've got everything figured out. I don't know whether they would be willing to try it or not, but I think I've got a pretty good plan, and I still disagree with the houses they send up north. Perhaps when I've finished my carvings, I'll try to get down south and bring my plans with me.

A Story of Starvation
Marion Tuu'luq*

Marion Tuu'luq is a well-known artist and craftswoman and, like many Inuit, she remembers vividly the traditional nomadic life she lived before she moved into Baker Lake in 1961. This true story illustrates the common saying that the old life was "a long walk on an empty stomach," but Mrs. Tuu'luq still prefers life on the land to that in the settlement. This piece appeared in Inuit Today *in 1977.*

I am going to recount a story that I am sure I have told over and over again in the past. It is not a happy story. At the time it took place, it looked as though we weren't going to survive. I will tell you some of those terrible events.

My name is Marion Tuu'luq, and my story goes back to the time when my father couldn't walk. My father was lame for as far back as I can remember into my childhood. We used to carry him on our backs when we travelled during the summer. In the winter, we pulled him on the qamutik.

One time, while we were at Tipyalik, there were no caribou to be found, and we became very hungry. Being just a young girl at the time, it didn't occur to me that the people I was with were very concerned and afraid.

While my brother Angutituaq and Oonark's husband were out searching for game, they came upon several traps, which brought them to some people. But they soon discovered that these people

*As told to Susan Tagoona

with the traps had been reduced to killing one of their dogs, since there was no game whatsoever in the area.

They skinned the dog, and when it was cooked, they told me to eat some of the meat. But I was so repelled by the meat of the dog that I was unable to eat. I really meant it with my whole heart when I said I didn't want to eat it, and they couldn't make me change my mind. I remember someone saying that the meat tasted just like a wolf.

When everyone was eating the dog meat, I too was given a piece. I tried to smell it, but I couldn't smell anything. Then, I put the piece in my mouth and I took it out again. I did this several times. I remember clearly how much I was repelled that day at the thought of eating a dog.

While the eating was going on, my father was lying down on the bed as usual. He was scarcely breathing. I didn't know then that the following day he would strangle himself with a rope, and we would have to leave him behind. When he was asked to eat, on that final day of his life, he refused. He didn't want to take even a sip of broth.

The next day, my brother Quenungnat and I were directed to go a little distance away from the igloo. We were told to stay there until someone called for us and we were ready to leave our camp. Of course, we wondered at the reason for this command. But we stayed as we were told until Nattaq, Quenungnat's mother, waved at us, signalling that it was now okay for us to return. It was then that I learned that my father had died and that I would not be seeing him again. I cried, for I loved my father very much. His name was Ekinilik.

Innakatsik, who was just a kid, even younger than myself, was asked to lead the way, but he didn't want to. So then, I was asked to lead and was told to follow the tracks on the snow.

While I was walking in the lead, I spotted a rock that was barely showing in the snow ahead of me. It indicated that a sled had passed by that spot only the day before. As I started to approach the rock, I heard the voice of my father say to me, "It is a cache, it is a cache." And here he had just died a short while before!

I started kicking at the rock, shouting "It's a cache! It's food!" And I would not leave the rock.

"There can't be anything around here. You wouldn't know of any caches around here, you are not able to know!" answered my brother Angutituaq in a scolding voice. But I just kept on kicking at the rock and shouting, "It's food! It's a cache!" For some reason, I just couldn't leave the rock alone.

"It's nothing. It can't be anything!" Angutituaq kept answering back at me.

Then the others started shovelling at the rock, and, true to my words, they uncovered—a cache! As we loaded it on our sled, it seemed as though we were stealing someone else's cache. But we didn't know of anyone who would have a cache, and we were threatened with starvation. We had sighted some fox traps the previous day, which probably belonged to the Akiliningmiut, and maybe the cache was theirs.

When we had loaded the meat on our sled, my father's voice again spoke to me: "Daughter, I don't want you to eat the liver and the heart of this caribou." I told him that I would do as he said.

After the men had made an igloo, I was allowed to feast on the meat which I had discovered. The men told me to eat all that I wanted. They fed me everything—the heart, the liver—everything! They told me that there would have been nothing to eat if it hadn't been for me.

The next day, when I woke up, I was unable to open my eyes. "What is the matter with her now? Look at her, she can't even

Marion Tuu'luq 123

open her eyes! Did somebody hurt you?" Nattaq shouted at me. It must have been because I had eaten the meat after my father had told me not to. Again, I heard the voice of my father warning me, "Daughter, do not eat the heart and the liver of the caribou."

"I forgot," I answered. No sooner had I said this than my eyes were opened.

When I try to tell this part of the story, I am not confused about the details. It is something I will never forget.

Later, there were no caribou at all. We didn't even see any caribou tracks. We were forced to live on dog meat. Killing and eating our dogs was the only way we could survive. As we travelled, we came across scraps of dried meat and the bones of caribou left over from the winter before, but they did not satisfy our hunger.

One day, Innakatsik went off on his own to search a nearby igloo for food. When he returned, he said he had discovered that it was full of dried meat. We all went straight to the igloo he had found. When we entered it, the people there just kept looking down and did not raise their heads. We were deeply disappointed, for there was no food there—nothing to eat at all. "Is there food?" asked my brother Angutituaq. But no one had the heart to answer him.

As we no longer had any dogs, we packed all our belongings on our backs, and we started to walk. Along the way, we caught a rabbit and ate it, and that was all we had to eat.

For a time, we kept on walking, but it was not long before we realized that we weren't going to run into any people. Instead, we decided to search for igloos. We came across two—one large, one small—and we looked for tracks around them, but there were none. It was bitterly cold by now, and there were frequent blizzards and storms, so we decided to return to the shelter of our old igloo. There was just a small group of us together at that time—Angutituaq, Tamalik and myself. Weak from starvation, we were forced to leave clothes, blankets and other belongings behind. I took only a blanket with me, and I wrapped it around my shivering body. When we lay down to sleep, I made sure that all my body was covered, and I had no trouble going to sleep.

Each time we awoke, we would force ourselves to start walking again. Angutituaq was close to starvation. We were just beginning to give up ourselves because of him, when we finally reached our old igloo.

Before we could enter the welcome shelter of the igloo, we had to dig a hole through the side to make a door. After our last stay there, we had sealed the door with snow to protect some skins we had left inside. Finally, we succeeded in digging ourselves an entrance way, but it was very narrow. Then, my brother said, "I think Tuu'luq should be able to squeeze in through." "It's too small!" I shouted back at him. But I tried to pass through the narrow hole, and at last I succeeded. Angutituaq followed behind me.

I don't know how many days we had wandered and nights we had slept before we reached our igloo. We had not had anything to eat for a long time, and we were very thin and nearly starved to death.

"I smell hide!" we all shouted out as we reached the inside of the igloo, for we found skins there that were to have been used for whips. We cut the skins in pieces and devoured them hungrily. Then we scraped up and ate some blood that we discovered on a block of snow. White people use plates to eat off—we used snow. There was a lot of blood on the snow plate, so we ate from that, and that was the way we survived.

Whenever Angutituaq came across little pieces of meat, he

offered them to me, even though I begged him to eat them himself instead. But he wanted so badly for me to eat.

It was a while before we felt we had gathered enough strength to leave the igloo again. We decided from then on that, if we wanted to eat, we would have to look for left-over caribou stomachs in abandoned caches. So, that is what we did. Sometimes we were lucky enough to come across caribou stomachs in old caches and we would eat their contents. Other times, we would find nothing and would return to our igloo and empty stomachs.

One time, Angutituaq and Oonark's husband decided to go out hunting for game. So Quenungnat and his brother went to look for a cache to provide the hunters with some food to take on their way. But the two men returned after just a short while to say that there were no caches left.

Angutituaq, however, said he knew of a place close by that he wanted to check. So we went to that place and discovered there what appeared to be a cache. Again, I started shouting—as I used to be very outspoken at that time—"It's a cache! It's a cache! It's a whole caribou!" One of the men answered me: "Your brother and I tried to find food, but we returned empty-handed because it had been moved to a different area. You know that. There couldn't be anything in here."

Still, we spent the whole day trying to shovel off the snow with a pana (Eskimo snow knife). "I smell a cache. It is a cache, and I know it hasn't been touched," I continued to insist. I think, by that time, the others were almost ready to give up. But I never used to think of how I was feeling. And the thing turned out to be a cache, after all.

We each loaded pieces of meat on our backs and prepared to return to the igloo. But we had scarcely moved more than a few feet away when we decided to stop right there and eat our fill. And did we ever eat! We chopped at the meat, pounded it, chipped and cracked it in halves with our snow knife. We had tried to walk with the meat on our backs, but we were so skinny by then, that we had no strength left for walking with such a weight to carry. So we ate the whole caribou, leaving only the neck and the head, which we took back with us.

After we reached our igloo, the men made plans to set out again to search for caribou stomachs on top of a hill. So we did, wandering further and further away. We walked the whole afternoon and didn't find a thing, so we decided to return home. All we had with us were the gun and the pana. We had left everything else we owned behind for we were too weak to carry anything with us. It was very hard for us. Every time I offered to carry the gun, my brother said no. I felt that, since I was the one with the most strength left, I should be the one to carry the gun.

Sometime later, we neared the igloo where we had been making our home. As we approached, we suddenly became aware of a group of people standing there. Oh, how frightened we were! We had finished off all their hides that were to have been used for making whips, and now they had come back for them.

"They've caught some caribou and they're bringing it back here!" Quenungnat was running and shouting at the same time. He was also trying to eat and getting scolded for his behaviour. I was still so afraid of what the men might do!

As it turned out, these hunters had caught some caribou and were returning to their overnight camp. They started to make themselves an igloo and I tried to help by cutting out blocks for them. My brother Angutituaq was still too weak from lack of food.

After the igloo was completed, Conark's husband started to work on the porch. But the men told him not to bother as they would be on their way again by the next day. Then, one of them said, "These people are not helping themselves to food. Get them something to eat."

That night, after all of us had eaten our fill, we started to tell stories. As usual, I found lots to laugh at. In those days, I used to laugh often and was very talkative. Now, everything seemed so funny.

Some of our group told how, each time they approached an igloo, they would yell through the ice window, "Is there anyone in there? Anyone in there?"

Nattaq said that, upon reaching our old igloo, they had spotted our fresh tracks in the snow, but there had been no one around. And Talluq had started to imagine that our dead bodies were in the porch. They had all looked around, then entered the igloo and found it empty. When they came out of the igloo, they saw us coming towards them, and they were so happy to see that we were all still together.

When Nattaq started to talk again about how she thought I might be dead and how she had searched the igloo looking for me, I started to laugh.

"This girl never runs out of laughs," Angutituaq said.

Remembering Old Times
Simon Arnaviapik

Like most northerners, Simon Arnaviapik of Pond Inlet had to turn his hand to many different jobs during his working years; he was a hunter, a sealer, a coal miner, a longshoreman, and finally an author. Along with most old Inuit, he considers legends and local history to be an essential part of the story of his life, so his reminiscences contain a great variety of material. Included in this narrative are his recollections of a fight involving Second-Mate ("Sakimeak") Robert Janes, a trader who was mysteriously murdered in the North. This piece was first published in Inuktitut *magazine in 1974.*

I began writing this on November 2nd, 1969. My name is Arnaviapik. Some people my age still use the old disc numbers that have been discarded. My number was E5-752. I am going to tell a story of my experiences.

I cannot remember exactly how old I was, but I do remember that it was summer when we used to go hunting caribou. I think it was the beginning of August. We were travelling from the salt water up on the mainland. I remember riding on top of the load which my father carried on his back. Sometimes I walked with my mother holding my hand.

There were six heads of families in our camp—my father Angutiyak, Kunuk, Kukuayuk, Tunga, Kasateak and Takauyuk. We would part in the summer, then meet again in the fall.

We would travel by land only at that time of the year. Walking and pulling our goods on a skin sled. First we would live by a lake in a tupik (skin tent) until we could move into an igloo (snow house). The men fished and shot caribou often. When our tupik was no longer required, my father would put it in the lake for several days. I saw that my father was making a wooden sled frame. I still remember how he pulled the tupik skins from the lake and stretched them flat on the ground and anchored them with rocks. Next he cut them into strips and tied the strips to both sides of the runners. He made holes for a cross bar. The cross bar was made from caribou antlers. It looked like a real sled even though some parts of it had once been our house.

Before we travelled, my mother made new parkas and other clothes for us. Then we went back to the coast. I think it was November when we arrived. The men went seal hunting and were lucky to catch some. They went hunting every day while we waited for the people from Iqajuak to come for us. When they came we returned with them and spent the winter there.

People who hunted the caribou with guns did not throw away their empty cartridges after using them. They made more bullets by mixing gunpowder and melting lead to make the balls. Two boxes of cartridges containing ten rounds each would last for the whole summer that way. Now there are twenty cartridges in each box and we do not have to reload them.

I remember when our people smoked before there was anything like cigarettes. They smoked using bone or metal pipes. They would use a flint to light their pipes. First they softened some paper, mixed gunpowder in hot water and put the black mixture on the paper. When the paper was dry they used it to light their pipes. When the spark from the flint fell on the paper it caught fire. They used real fire when meat was cooking.

I also remember living in Iqajuak, although I do not know what year it was. There was a white man there called Sakimeak who was unhappy because his ship did not arrive. I often watched him walking around the seashore, eating kelp. The ship finally came a year after we had moved to Tulukak. This Sakimeak had moved to Saneruak and then to Tulukak. Sakimeak and an Inuk came on foot to Tulukak, carrying fox skins. The white man went to the ship and while on board got into a fight with a man from Sanieruak. They fought and the white man won. The second mate intervened and put him in his place. The captain told the white man to leave and he went back to shore.

My mother and I were alone on shore when Sakimeak came to our shelter. He was weeping. I was frightened at first but he stayed with us that night.

The next morning the captain of the ship and some other white people came ashore to look for Sakimeak. They found him with us and they talked to him for a long time. They told him that he could not travel with them on the ship. They said there was a war on and because the man was a German they could not take him. They told him to go by dogteam to Churchill when winter came.

When I was perhaps four or five years old, my elder sister and I went with my father to the trading post early in the winter. We were at Tulukak then. We rode on the sleigh and I remember it was very early in the morning when we arrived at the post. Though my sister and I were frightened, we decided to follow my father into the store. The people gave us food to eat and when we were leaving a white lady gave me a small spoon. I was happy to receive it.

After we left Tulukak, we visited my aunt's house at Keminik. This was a happy time for me because I did not know she was my aunt. Then we went back to our old camp at Iqajuak. I remember it was there that Aleanakulook's wife died. This was the first time that a person I knew died. My grandmother became very ill too and she died. She was not very old.

Simon Arnaviapik 131

It was spring again when we went west to hunt caribou. When summer came, we walked inland. I believe it was the end of July. We hunted the caribou there for about three months.

Our people used to run out of tobacco often. The men used to mix their tobacco to make it go farther. Sometimes they would smoke small leaves. They even smoked with feathers. I remember how they used to smell.

In the fall we went back to the coast by dogteam. We used to light our lamps with caribou fat. When we reached the sea the men would hunt at the seal holes. When we had seal fat it was much better. The flame in the lamps was bright red and not as smoky as when using caribou fat.

When we were on the coast a dogteam came for us from Iqajuak. The drivers told us that there were traders at Pond Inlet and my father decided we should go with them. We had to stop several times on the way. When we arrived we found there were four white men at Pond Inlet—Big Kapitie, his clerk, an interpreter and a policeman, they all lived together at the Hudson's Bay Company house. A lady invited us in and gave us food. They gave the children candy and the older people tobacco.

We stayed at Pond Inlet until after Christmas at which time we left for Igloolik by dogteam. The policeman and an interpreter came with us on the journey. We carried merchandise, guns and ammunition for trading at Igloolik. Besides us there was another Inuk with a five-dog team who came with us.

It was spring when we got back from Igloolik. We returned to Pond Inlet with a light load of fox skins. It was much lighter than the load we had taken with us. We bought supplies and other goods to take back to our camp at Iqajuak.

When summer came again the *Atik* (the C.G.S. *Arctic*) arrived with a policeman. When they left they took a man named

Keugayuk with them as a prisoner. It was getting dark early when the *Nassikupee* (the S.S. *Nascopie)* arrived.

The next fall they asked my father to go to the Hudson's Bay post when the ice was set. The white men hired the Inuit to gather fuel for their stoves (from the coal deposits near Pond Inlet). In the winter there was fuel only at the store. When they ran out of it, they went to get some more, hauling it by dogteam.

The post manager left when break-up came and his clerk took over at Pond Inlet. When fall came again people from Igloolik and Pond Inlet sacked up more coal. Spring came and they loaded it on boats. My family stayed with the traders all summer. After freeze-up the manager, Neegasee, decided to go to Igloolik by dogteam. My father and his family, Akumalik and his family, including his children, Idlout and Eitokudso, went along with the trader.

In December that year the trader wanted to return by land to Pond Inlet. My father did not wish to go that way because he was not familiar with the route. The white man said that the map showed that it was a shortcut and that we could get there more quickly. My father pointed out that if they attempted to go that way at that time of the year they might all starve. It was a poor time—there was little food for humans and less for the dogs. The trader still persisted and Akumalik took the trader's side in the argument. They outvoted my father. He at last agreed to go but still warned them of the danger.

When the journey began the days were already very short. There were no familiar landmarks to follow. Soon we ran out of food and were very hungry. Some of the party became so hungry they wanted to eat their dogs. My father said that if they had only listened to him and travelled by the sea ice they would have seal meat for themselves and the dogs.

The people were sorry to do it, but soon found it necessary to kill some of the dogs if they were to survive. They boiled the dogs and ate them. They wanted my father to turn around and take them back to Igloolik. There was no more kerosene for the stoves. My father knew that turning around would mean certain death. He told them that they had to go on. He left them and travelled alone ahead of the dogs. He was searching for a hunting camp. He told the people he would find help and send it to them.

My father knew he could travel much faster if he went alone, but against his wishes, his brother-in-law came too. But he slowed the pace down because he kept lagging behind and my father would have to wait for him.

My father reached sea ice. He could tell by the signs around that he had gone past an Inuit hunting camp. He waited for his companion but he did not come for a long time. When he finally arrived, my father told him that they had reached salt water. The man did not believe it until he tasted the snow. My father told him to look for seal holes while he went to look for the hunting camp that must not be far away. The man was just too cold and hungry to hunt, so my father left him, promising to send someone for him if he found help.

My father arrived at an Inuit sealing camp during the night. The men had just returned from hunting. My father told them what had happened. The men harnessed their dogs and left to look for the rest of the party. They followed his tracks. They found the people who had been walking slowly for two days. They would have frozen to death had they stopped walking. They were very weak. They then knew the wisdom of my father's words. If he had not left them, all would have perished.

The Inuit often talked about the white man who had been with them and how he had cooked the dog meat and eaten it while it was still almost raw. A year later he was replaced by a new manager and my father took him to Clyde River to be the trader. My father took me to Clyde River with him. There was one trader there and an Inuk whose name was Matuk. His wife was called Eevaluapik. They had two sons—one called Miee and a younger one called Moses. In the spring we often went seal hunting with the men. I had a .22 calibre rifle, but Miee was not allowed to shoot.

When summer came to Clyde River, the ship *Nassikupee* arrived. I was growing up. They asked me to go on the ship to help. We went to Pond Inlet to unload and left again. My father became foreman of the unloading gang. I was surprised to see that we were going to Resolute Bay. There were three men with us from Cape Dorset—Pootoogook, Eitoolook and Pitseolak. That was in 1927 or 1928, I cannot be sure which.

Our manager at that time had six Inuit with him who came from Labrador. They wanted to become trappers at a place where no one lived and hunt for the Company. Some of the people got off at Arctic Bay but we stayed until we reached Pond Inlet.

That winter we caught many white fox and in the spring took the pelts to Pond Inlet. A supply ship arrived and they asked my father if he would go aboard as a guide. I went along too and we went to Resolute Bay and past it in a small boat. We unloaded lumber and supplies at Arctic Bay and other places, always unloading lumber.

We travelled all summer. One man, Attagutaaluk, and his wife Attuak (she is still living) came aboard. We stopped at a small island. The season was getting late and the weather was bad. We were going very slowly but suddenly we stopped. We were stranded on a sand bar. The water was only fifteen inches deep. They tried to take the ship backwards but it would not go.

While the tide was out we got off the boat. The men unloaded the supplies and lumber. It took nearly all day. In spite of this the boat tipped over in the evening. Oil drums were attached to the bottom of the boat with ropes. When the tide came in, the boat started to float. Then began the job of reloading it.

Next we went to Gjoa Haven on King William Island. We were to spend the winter there with the trader and his clerk. Our family were the only Inuit. My father and the trader travelled a lot that winter. During one absence, people from Netsilik arrived. I was very frightened when I saw them for the first time. Their way of talking reminded me of eider ducks just before they learn to fly. They were "the people of the place possessing seal" and the only ones who were still living by the old ways without southern equipment which we were now almost accustomed to using.

My father and the trader were away for a long time. The ice was about to freeze up when they finally returned. They had attempted to go to every camp to trade and encourage the people to come to Gjoa Haven where the new house had been built.

I always liked to go hunting with my father. It was from him and Attagutaaluk that I learned how to trap fox. Once when I was hunting with Angnateak, it was growing dark. He said to me, "Look at that big polar bear!" I thought he was trying to fool me and I did not believe him. But when I looked to one side there it was and very close. I was going to shoot at it but the dogs were excited and I had to control them. Angnateak started to run after the bear. I went after him as soon as I tied up some of the dogs. There were so many tracks that I soon lost Angnateak. The dogs broke loose and I felt like crying because I could not handle them. It was now very dark and I could not see or hear Angnateak. Finally he found me. He had not been able to shoot the bear but I was happy to see him. We had lost a few dogs. When we returned to camp we found that some of the other men had killed a bear. I was sad that we were not so lucky.

In winter I always went hunting with Angnateak. He was my brother-in-law and my best friend. Sometimes when we were alone we would wrestle. He was very strong and I would try not to show it when he hurt me. If I cried he would feel bad.

In the spring we often had visitors at the store in Gjoa Haven. Some of them stayed for a while, camping nearby. They were happy people. One man who stayed was from Netsilik. After break-up we took him to Arctic Bay. On our way back we planned to stop at Pond Inlet, but had to return because of the thick ice. We returned to spend the winer at Gjoa Haven again. There, white man's food was available.

In 1929 two boats came to Gjoa Haven. One stayed for the winter. Fox were plentiful that year. All the white people ran out of food, even sugar, tea and milk. The white people lived in our camp and went hunting with us. They were glad for the spring when the ducks, geese and other birds came and they could go fishing.

After break-up, a small boat came near the shore with supplies. Food was the first thing taken off and then oil and lumber. After we loaded our boat we took the supplies into the post. My father left with the boat but I stayed with the white people. I worked with them and ate with them. I tried hard to learn their language. It was very hard and I still do not know it. I returned to Pond Inlet in the spring of 1930. It was then I killed my first seal. There were many of them laying out on the ice in the warm sun.

I used to be very excited when I first started going out alone by dogteam. One spring I went out from Pond Inlet to get my uncle and some other men to help gather coal for the post at Pond Inlet. On our way back we stopped to hunt seal for food. We were travelling on the shore ice when the weather became stormy. There were times when we could not see the dogs in front of us. My uncle decided we should stop. We thought we were lost and had moved too far out on the ice. After a while my uncle walked some distance to see if he could discover any landmarks. When he returned he told us we had to go against the wind. It was very slow. The women and children stayed on the komotiks. It was very difficult and sometimes the dogs stopped because their eyes were blinded by the snow and frost. They would not move again until it was removed. When we finally reached land we took the seal catch off to lighten our load. The snow was too fine and blowing to build a house with. We made a small shelter and boiled water for tea. While we rested the wind died down. We knew we were on the right trail. We travelled through the night and reached Pond Inlet in the morning.

In the spring of 1930 the ice extended far out and did not melt all summer. We unloaded lumber that arrived for the Hudson's Bay Company. We used six dogteams to haul it from the ship to the post. The work was hard and the hours long. We would come home late at night and get up early in the morning. After we had brought the timber the manager had us pile it ready to load again the next spring to be sent to other trading posts. After we finished our work in the spring they threw a big party for us. It was a happy time for everyone. The traders were good to the Inuit. They gave us food, baking powder, flour, sugar, tea and many other things.

The Hudson's Bay Company employed our people to dig stove coal. They paid us fifty cents for a bag. My father was in charge of this work until he died in 1953. Then I took over his job. My brother, Takugak and I always managed to fill more bags than the others. When a man filled twenty bags he would receive ten dollars. After some time fifty cents for a bag did not seem like enough for all the work that had to be done. The manager agreed to give us eighty cents. By the end of the season I managed to convince the manager that we should have still more. He agreed to one dollar a bag and that was the limit. I was happy about this. There were eleven men digging and bagging coal.

In 1957 we lived on an island during the summer. Then we moved to Qimmivik. I became very ill during February, but by March I was feeling much better. I had become very thin but soon regained my strength. While I was sick my children caught seals in nets. We were never hungry because we were the only family living there and we did not have to share our catch.

In March, 1958, an airplane landed at our camp. It was the Royal Canadian Mounted Police officer. He was taking a doctor to all the camps. Our camp was located on a river and I had caught enough fish to last us for the winter. We had no seal oil for our lamps so we spent a great deal of time in darkness. We did not mind this as long as we were not hungry. I had a stove made out of an old oil drum. The snow was so deep that it was impossible to travel. We were unable to get seal because the deep snow had covered their breathing holes. We used part of our sleigh for fuel. The deep snow lasted until March, 1959. It became very windy. Finally we were able to leave to find a place where we could get seal. We set our tents up on a small island. I was hunting rabbits when I took a severe cramp in my leg and couldn't walk. We were just about out of everything when some people came for us. We returned to Pond Inlet in April and got some work from the post manager. I still had trouble walking.

When summer came I went fishing again. We were alone in the camp then because my brother had taken my oldest son on a caribou hunt. I went to the river during the first week of August to prepare our fishing ground. Every year you have to set up new stones to divert the fish into a small trap. The fish were all going up stream and I caught a great many and hung them up to dry.

Near the end of August a police boat came for us. They said

that the Canadian Government Ship *C.D. Howe* was coming to Pond Inlet and that they were taking X-rays of all the people to check for tuberculosis. We stopped fishing and left with the police. It was the middle of September before we got back to the river. The dogs that we had left behind had ruined our fishing dam trying to feed themselves. We would have only what we had dried and cached out of their reach.

That was a good winter for hunting. We hunted seal and set nets through the ice. I caught one hundred and three foxes and in the spring bought a radio and an outboard motor.

In 1966 we moved to Pond Inlet because the Government built a big school for our children and a number of houses for the people. We moved into our house right away. I was so excited that I did not sleep well for a few nights. I was worried that we would not be able to keep it clean, but it did not take long to get used to it. It was quite a surprise when a man first came to take out our toilet bucket. Women had always done this work. Later another man came with blocks of fresh water ice for drinking. We are grateful to the Government for all they have done for us. We have a much better life than we ever had before.

Ever since I can remember, the world has been changing. The weather seems to be getting milder. I often wonder if the animals are getting scarce in the North. I know the fish are scarcer around Pond Inlet. I remember when people used to catch a lot of fish in summer. They used to fill their boats in a short time. Now this does not happen anymore. No wonder the fish are getting scarce. Since the white man came he has never stopped fishing. When the traders, missionaries and police were using dogs they used to get enough fish to last their teams all winter. They only fish for themselves now. Inuit only fished for food but we have started using nets more now and boats that can take farther out.

At one time there were few animals at Pond Inlet during the winter. Many people went hungry. Now the caribou seem to be coming back. They started coming back in 1961 and now there are quite a few.

I used to listen to Kudlooteak, an old man, talking about the caribou. He said it was unusual that there were no caribou but that they would be back in time. I think the older people knew a lot about these things. Kudlooteak was certainly right.

In earlier days when the Inuit went hunting, they would share the kill with all their neighbours. If they were out hunting seal and a man shot one, he would go to his companion and get him to help clean it. Then they would share the liver, meat and fat. When they had enough they would freeze the rest and take it home to their families. When they got home they would invite the other families and the men would eat raw meat. The women would take some of the meat and cook along with some seal blood. Everyone shared in this meal. Anything that was left over would be eaten for breakfast by the hunters before they went out again.

Except in the winter people always ate outside. Before they had primus stoves it took quite a while to make tea. They carried water in caribou skin bags. This left the water lukewarm. When fresh meat was running low they would melt ice and mix it with seal blood. This was a very good soup and good for little children.

In the spring we would take our dogs and hunt for baby seals that would be laying on the ice in the warm sun. Sometimes we went for days without sleep while looking for them. In the summer the young men went out with kayaks to hunt caribou when they were crossing streams.

The Inuit on the coast used their kayaks to hunt whale. When a whale was caught it was shared with all the people in the camp. The lucky hunter got the biggest portion. Besides the white whale and the narwhal, sometimes we were fortunate and got square flipper seals. The skin of this seal is very good for making lines and ropes. The man who shot the seal always got the middle part of the skin. This means a longer rope. The meat was shared among the hunters.

When the caribou hunters returned they would gather the hides and choose the ones they wanted for clothing. Two hides were needed for a man's parka. The meat was distributed around the camp. One of the older men was usually in charge.

When a man had tobacco he would share it with his companions. This was the old kind of chewing tobacco. He would cut a plug of it into small pieces, press them into a pipe and when it was lit, pass it around to each man in turn for a few puffs.

In the spring when seals were plentiful, the skins were fashioned into containers for storing lamp oil. This was done by making holes around the outside edge of the skin. Then a line was threaded through the holes to draw the skin together to make a pouch. In those days, Inuit made most of their own utensils and tools. Today this is not so. Most of them are bought.

The Inuit men were much stronger and swifter in the past. It was not uncommon for a man to outrun a caribou. Men were careful about displaying their strength because it sometimes displeased the witch doctors. It was said that the witch doctor would get jealous and could cause the death of a man. Now there are no witch doctors and the men are not as strong as they used to be.

Spring time was the best time for polar bear hunting. The older men felt sad at this time of the year because they could remember when they were young and strong enough to join in the most exciting hunting there was to be had.

The story I have told involves me personally in part and the other stories were told to me. My eyesight is very poor now and I have probably made many mistakes with my pencil. However, I hope you have been able to follow my story without too much difficulty. Now that I am older, I only occasionally hunt seal through the ice. My son is the one who provides me with fresh meat.

I would like to speak on another subject now. Before the missionaries came, we prayed to the spirits. Now they have converted us to Christianity. We are very thankful to the missionaries who taught us to believe in God. I know that the Inuit are and will in future generations be good Christians because we believe that God can and has helped us in a great many ways.

Here are a few short stories that you will find interesting. When my father was a small boy, he often went seal hunting with the men. On one of these trips the wind came up strong. This caused the ice to break up and they drifted out into open water. When they were out some distance, the ice-pan started to break up. Fortunately they were close enough to an iceberg and were able to climb up on to it. There was a lot of snow on the iceberg and they were able to build a shelter. It was very wet but it was a shelter. There was an invisible monster living in this iceberg and when the iceberg looked as though it would break up, Sakayuk, one of the men, said that the monster would not let this happen because it would drown as well. Finally, the sea ice froze into a solid mass again. When they left the iceberg it began to break up.

This is another story. Two years later when my father was bigger and living on an island and there was plenty of food, he went to the mainland to hunt caribou with a man and his wife and an old unmarried lady. When they were ready to leave and return home to the island, the old lady who had been doing some sewing told them she had forgotten her ulu (woman's knife). She ran back for it.

Simon Arnaviapik 143

When she did not return to the boat one of the men went to look for her. He saw tracks that showed she was running into the interior. He followed for a while but she was nowhere in sight. Finally they had to leave without her. She was found much later. She had walked all the way from near Pond Inlet to Clyde River. It is still considered impossible to do this. The lady's name was Emudluk Aduaruluk.

I believe it was in 1933 that I got married. We moved near Pond Inlet for the winter with my father. When I was trapping for fox I would be away by myself for long days. In February that year we moved to where there were seals. We had no food. I returned after for my traps. Fox were plentiful that year and I stayed away for more than a week. While I was trapping my father went with a policeman to help him get to Pond Inlet. The next year, I think it was 1934, we all moved closer to Pond Inlet. The first year of our marriage was very difficult now that I look back on it.

When summer came we went caribou hunting for the months of August and September. We needed a supply of skins for clothing. My father stayed on the coast to hunt seal but he did not get many because of bad weather. Food was low when winter came. We went to get some meat we had cached away earlier but it had become rotten. We were hungry but still had a hard time to eat the bad meat. When we ran completely out of food we moved to Evalak's camp. There were many people there and they had plenty of food. They gave us some and we returned home and shared one seal.

Later on some people came with my father to fetch us. I was the only one with dogs. It was a long journey and they began to die of starvation. My wife and I got behind the other people. My dogs were down to three and I had to help them pull the sleigh. We lost our way. In the morning of the second day that we were alone, we had nothing but warm water for our stomachs. It was in December, the month of Christmas. The days were very short. I was just going to abandon our equipment and take our blankets and walk. I thought I could reach people more quickly by walking. Suddenly I heard dogs barking in the darkness and my dogs raised their heads. We listened. I could tell it was my father by the sounds he used to make his dogs go faster. It was very dark although it was morning. I shouted with all my strength to let my father know where we were.

We could not have gone farther with the sleigh. I had used the cross bar for fuel. We had taken nothing but warm water for three days. The sound of my father's team coming was the greatest sound I had ever heard. We were almost in tears.

When we returned to our people they had lots of food. They also gave us dogs so I could go seal hunting again. We were at Arctic Bay.

When the sun came out again after the long winter a trader and a policeman came from Pond Inlet. We went back with them for a short time. We thought Arctic Bay might have more game so we came back. There were many dogteams now. Game continued to be scarce. We got very few caribou in the summer, and when freeze-up came, very few seals through the ice. Sometimes we left early in the morning without anything to eat and would stay hungry until someone harpooned a seal. Our dogs were thin but we did not have any starve to death. Things were getting better.

In 1936 we trapped fox and seal. It was pleasant in the month of March so we travelled to Pond Inlet to trade. The people had all run out of tobacco. I did not smoke, but I sure wanted to have a cup of tea.

In 1936 three people died. They were all adults. When we arrived at Pond Inlet the people asked us to stay with them. The trader hired my father to work for him again. My father-in-law and I moved to a place near Pond Inlet. I was able to hunt caribou that summer and when freeze-up came went to Pond Inlet for supplies. There was another trader in the area. There were very few foxes that winter but we did get a lot of fish.

The next year my wife and I were living all alone near Pond Inlet. Someone made a trip out to find us and tell me that the Hudson's Bay Company supply ship was coming and they needed me. I worked for the Company all that summer. In the fall I asked if I could return to my traps because all the signs looked like a good year for fox.

In the summer of 1940 three of us went sailing in my boat. I did not have a motor, but had rigged a canvas sail. We were hunting walrus. There were many walrus on a small island. We only got three of them because of the high wind. Later we shot two polar bears. On our way back it was very windy and the waves were high. There were many walrus in the water around us. We shortened our sail to keep from upsetting until we came to a point where we could anchor for the night. I guess we were lucky to make it back to our camp the next day.

There were now three of us, all friends, working and hunting together. I had one child, and the other men each had two children. Our wives helped each other with the children while we did the hunting. One summer we ate a lot of mushrooms because caribou were scarce. We decided to go inland. One morning I woke up early. I woke up my companions so we could get an early start. We left our families sleeping. I was ahead quite a bit when I saw eight caribou feeding across a stream. We got six caribou out of the eight. We were wet and shivering from crossing the stream but we were so very happy. Our wives set up camp near the stream and we carried the meat across to them. We had eaten only mushrooms and fungus for a week. What a feast we had!

Hunting improved and for the first week of August we shot caribou nearly every day. Our wives were busy cleaning hides. We rounded up all our dogs and got them ready for the coming winter.

When hunting is good you have to keep going. With one companion I set out one day in search of four caribou that I had seen in the distance. When we saw them again they were on the other side of what seemed a small stream. The water was much deeper than we expected and we nearly drowned. My friend lost his packsack and his gun. It was getting dark and we had no way to make a fire. We just had to huddle down and try to sleep. It was so cold I thought we would freeze. As soon as there was a little light we got up and started running to get warm. Suddenly we saw a herd of caribou and forgot our discomfort. I shot ten of them and my companion took my rifle and got ten more. After this I began to skin the animals while my friend went to bring our dogs. He was gone a long time for we had not realized how far we had run. We were strong and healthy in those days. What a load of hides, fat, sinew and meat we brought home! All the dogs were loaded down and we each had all we could carry. We found an easier way to cross the stream and reach the camp where the women waited for us.

We reached the coast in September and there was already a heavy snowfall. During the summer we had gathered so many caribou—fifty-five—that our loads were heavy and the journey to the coast took two weeks. We stayed on the coast for a while and when the ice froze, continued to Pond Inlet to trade and see my father.

When it was time to leave Pond Inlet again and go to my trapping camp, I asked my sister if she could come with us and she agreed. There were three dogteams in our party. I had a long sled and fourteen fine dogs. On the trip I harpooned a white whale and loaded it whole on our already heavy sled. My family were all riding on the sled and I was running ahead of the dogs. It was just growing dark when we hit a patch of thin ice and the sled began to sink. The dogs couldn't pull it. I ran back to my family but the ice kept breaking under me. I was praying as I worked to try and save them. I got my footing on some broken but floating ice and threw the end of my long dog whip to my wife. She tied it around her waist. She tried to run toward me but kept sinking in the broken ice. I pulled and pulled and finally got her to safe ice. She was chattering with the cold. I threw the whip back to my sister and pulled her in the same way.

The sled was lighter now and by adding my strength to that of the dogs, I was able to save our sled which was piled with everything we owned. I quickly unloaded it and piling my family on it raced through the night to where our camp was. We reached it in early morning. There were people there and they were all asleep. I awakened a man and his wife. Their names were Malaku and Kidlapik. His wife changed my wife's and sister's clothes which were frozen solid on the outside. We stayed with them for two days before our things were dry. Then I returned for the supplies I had left on the shore ice.

Long ago one fox skin would bring three dollars. We trapped very hard. A seal skin was a dollar and you got the same price for baby seal killed in the spring. Looking back now, it seemed we always worked hard to stay alive. Now that I am old I am grateful for a warm house and a son who provides me with country food. Once I never stopped travelling but now I am content to stay home.

In the Spring
When the Sun Never Sets
Lucy Evaloardjuak

This poem is a first attempt, written by Lucy Evaloardjuak of Pond Inlet after she had discussed various forms of writing with James McNeill, a literature development specialist. The poem was printed originally in the Eskimo language in Inuktitut *and appeared first in English in the magazine* Intercom *in 1969.*

In the spring when the sun never sets
And when calm glassy waters roamed the
morning seas,
Oh, those were the happy times.

When the birds and seals,
Lived only for playing,
Oh, those were the happy times.

When we would stay up all night,
Looking for birds' nests,
Oh, those were the happy times.

When the sun began to warm the
morning air
And my sister could no longer keep her
eyes open,
Oh, those were the happy times.

When I, too, fought the coming of sleep,
But my dreams would win in the end,
Oh, those were the happy times.

Story of Inukshuk
Mark Kalluak

Mark Kalluak was editor of the newspaper Keewatin Echo *for a number of years and is now in business in the North. He edited and illustrated* How Kabloonat Became and Other Legends. *In this piece, taken from the* Echo *for May 1973, he tells one of his own stories.*

I am an inukshuk, a lonely figure overlooking a lake below me. In time where memory is wiped from young and old, a frail, struggling form in fur picked me up off the ground, placed me here on a rock and said, "May you ever point to the fishes under this lake as long as there is winter and summer."

I have lost count of how many people visited me. As many times as you can count your fingers and toes, people have knelt above me to consult which way I point to fishes in a lake below me. Many lives were saved as a result of my faithfulness to the frail man's command.

I have been through the many terrors of the blinding snow storms, but have kept my post.

The Many Lives of Anakajuttuq
Joe Panipakuttuk

In 1944 Joe Panipakuttuk took his family and dogs and boarded the RCMP *boat* St. Roch *for the historic trip through the Northwest Passage. His contributions to the success of that voyage were later recognized when he was posthumously awarded the Polar Medal for Arctic Discoveries, but he will probably be best remembered as a storyteller and writer. Here is his version of a famous Inuit legend.*

First Anakajuttuq was a cloud but since a cloud will not stand up, he soon became tired of being a cloud and turned into a caribou. He ate black soil and became very thin.

The rest of the caribou were fat, so one day he asked, "What do you eat to keep fat? I eat a lot but I am thin."

He showed the other caribou what he ate and they said, "Eat caribou moss. You see the moss we are talking about is yellowish. Also eat a bit of the moss that forms on the rocks."

So Anakajuttuq started to eat caribou moss and became fat. He was now happy about his appearance, but when the other caribou played games in racing, he was always last. Again he asked, "How do you run to be so fast?"

They said, "Take long steps and try to keep your hair straight." So he did what he was told. When the caribou were playing games he joined in and kept up with no trouble.

Soon the migrating season came and the caribou were on their way to where they would spend the winter. They came to a lake and stopped to feed near it. While they were eating, one of the caribou saw hunters far away. They ran to the lake with all their might, but there was enough daylight left and the hunters killed many caribou.

Anakajuttuq was afraid to go into the water. He kept walking back and forth along the lake and the hunters were coming closer to him all the time. Finally another caribou told him to go in and cross the lake. He was swimming as hard as he could to survive, but the hunters were gaining on him. Finally one caught up with him and thrust down his harpoon. He tried not to think about the pain there would be when the harpoon went into him, but it was nothing but an itchy feeling and everything he could see became black.

When he regained consciousness he was a wolf. He chased caribou, but he could never keep up. He would catch up with the pack when the caribou was all eaten. Again he became thin when the rest of the wolves were fat. One day when the wolves were again chasing caribou, Anakajuttuq (knowing he would be last) shouted to the rest "Leave some meat for me when you get your catch."

He caught up and ate the left overs. Then he asked the eldest of the pack, "How do you run fast to catch a caribou?"

The old wolf said, "When you're running, try to kick the sky."

He tried kicking on the next chase and it worked. He kept up with the rest and ate with them. In a little while he was able to catch caribou alone and he became fat and happy.

One day, he came to a large igloo. The door was not closed and there was no one inside. At the back, there was a piece of meat and when he saw it he became hungry. He walked up to it, took it in his jaws and headed for the door. Suddenly the doorway closed, and then he heard a noise outside on top of the igloo. Something was trying to make a hole in the ceiling. He was frightened and thought he smelled smoke, but it was really the scent of a man. So the man made the hole in the ceiling and held up his spear. Anakajuttuq could not bear to think of the pain so he closed his eyes. The man speared him and he died again.

Later in his existence he became a seal. He was thin until the other seals told him to eat sea worms.

Winter came and each seal had a breathing hole. Above they could hear sounds of hunters looking for seals. They went to their breathing holes and above they could see people looking down with no sign of a smile on their face and making no sound. Anakajuttuq went to his breathing hole and when the man was about to harpoon him he swam away. He noticed that some of the seal holes were dark and some were light. The dark seal holes were where the poor hunters waited and the bright ones were where the good hunters waited out of sight.

Anakajuttuq couldn't hold his breath any longer so he went up and he saw the face of the hunter who harpooned him. He tried to break the hair (harpoon line) that was attached to him, but with no success. The next thing he knew he was being cut up. One piece of his flesh was taken home by a woman to her igloo. This woman did not go out early in the morning and she did not comb her hair early. He did not feel at home in this igloo, so his spirit left and went to another igloo. The next woman he lived with was much different. She went out early in the morning and combed her hair. He felt at home and stayed with her. At times he saw different faces peeking in, searching for a wife.

The igloo in which he stayed was very small and uncomfortable and after a while he started to go out. The air outside was cold. When he felt the cold, he tried to say how cold it was but he could only make the crying sound of an infant. No matter how hard he tried to speak, the only sound he made was the sound of a baby crying.

154   *Joe Panipakuttuk*

Later in life, when he grew up, he had a song that went like this:

Although I tried hard to speak,
the only sound I could make was Ungaa.
Although I tried hard to say I am cold,
I only cried.

Cup and Ball Game: Ajagarniq
Jeanne Arnainuk

Ajagarniq is a game of skill in which you tie a sharp stick or bone to a rabbit skull or a caribou vertebra. The object is to get the point of the stick into a hole in the bone. The game is often accompanied by a chant or song, much as skipping or ball bouncing games are in other parts of the world. The bone must be tossed on and then off the stick for every action named in the chant. Jeanne Arnainuk recalled the words for this game for Inummarit *in 1972.*

This game can be played by two or more people. The first who succeeds in passing the stick through the hole knocks out his opponent. When the opponent succeeds in passing the stick through, he comes back to life, rises, and in turn knocks out his opponent. He pushes him to make him slip, he slips 1,2,3,4,5,6,7,8,9,10 (10 passes in a row), he falls in water, he sinks, he touches bottom, he calls the seaweeds, they turn towards him, they get up, they come, 1, 2, 3, 4, 5, 6. Here they are, they reach him, and bend over him. When the other person passes the

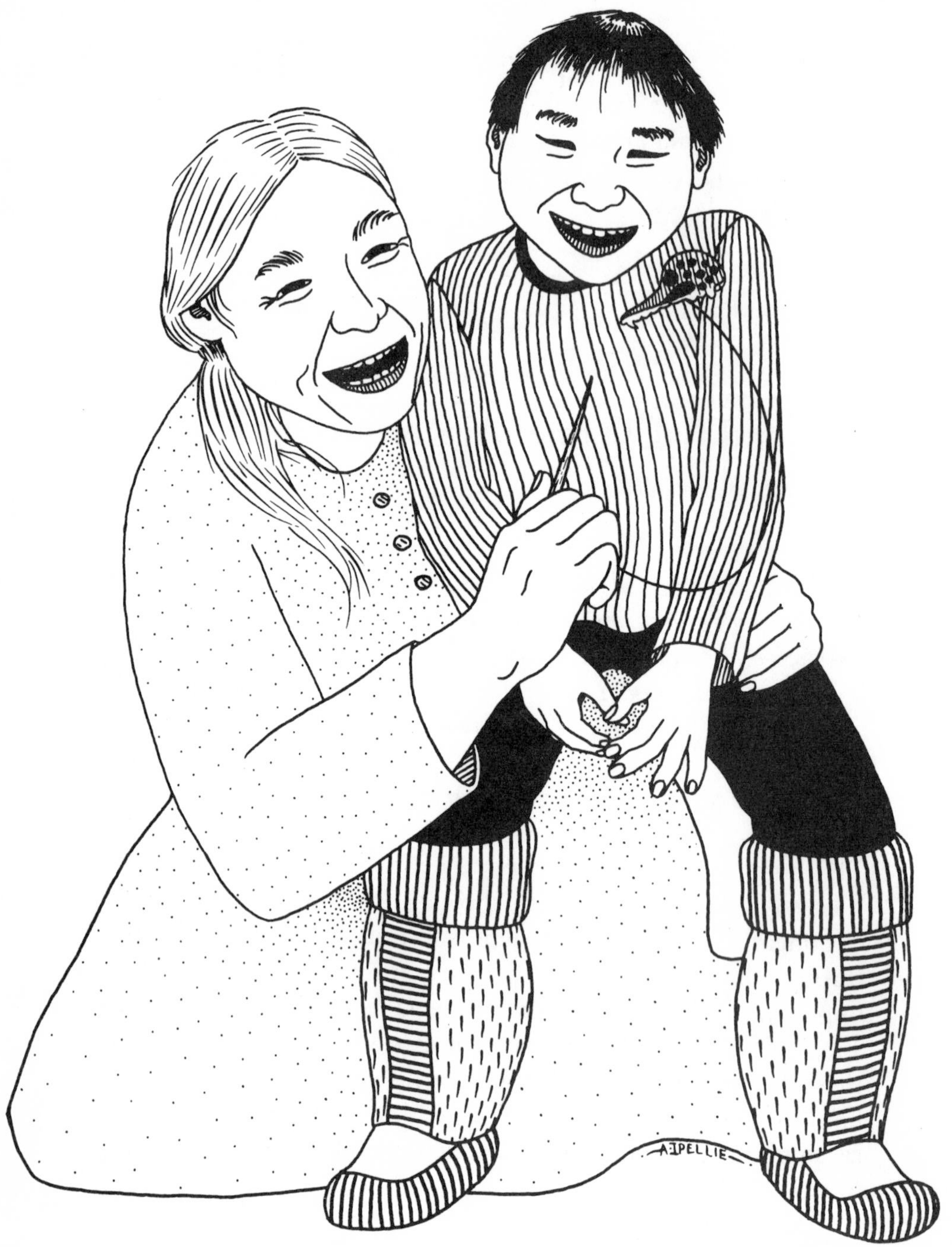
A·IPELLIE

stick once again, he whips the weeds, and whips until they leave at 5 (5 passes in a row). But if his opponent passes his stick, the seaweeds come back and reach the other one once again at 5. They bow before him, they chew him, they eat him, they eat, and eat, and eat on, they crack the bones, and crack the bones, they scrape off the bits of meat. When everything is scraped off and done, they leave 1,2,3,4,5,6,7,8,9,10 (10 successful passes in a row). They vomit, and they have vomited, he is covered with vomit, he has become like sand, he has become loathsome. However, if the opponent passes his stick through, when they start to eat him he can make the weeds vomit. He picks up the parts of his body which had been eaten, and when he has them all he can come back to life. The one that has been vomited cannot come back to life until he has reached the last stage and has become refuse.

The one who has lost comes out from under the pile of refuse. When he appears, the one who has won calls his opponent who answers. He sits down, he holds his hand towards his parka, takes it, puts it over his head, his head shows at the hood, he puts a sleeve on, then the other sleeve, he takes his pants, passes a leg through, then the other leg, he pulls it up to the belt, he sits down, he holds his hands towards his boots, takes them, he puts one leg through, then the other, puts a boot on, then the other, he drops down to the floor, he goes to take his mitts, holds out his hands to them, takes them, puts one on, then the other, he goes to get his knife, holds his hand towards it, takes it and goes towards the door, he cuts the door out, puts it aside, he bends down, goes through the porch and out.

He goes towards the shed, opens it, holds out his hand towards the things he will pack on his back. Takes this, packs it, goes towards his harpoon, holds out his hand, takes it and leaves. He walks, passes in front of the dump, goes across the first crack on

Jeanne Arnainuk 157

the ice, then the middle crack, and the last one. He scans the horizon, looks here and there, he perceives something, he sees it, he goes towards what he has seen, he walks and reaches it. He unpacks, bends his bow and shoots (it is only if he succeeds in passing the stick through by twirling from this side to that, that he may shoot). He strikes his quarry with his arrows, then he goes towards it, reaches it, draws out an arrow from the animal's body, then another. He stretches the animal on its back, he cuts it, and cuts it again, he skins it and takes the skin away, then he arranges the meat, then he ties a string around it to pull it along, then he pulls it along and goes, passes a crack, then the middle one, then the last, passes in front of the dump, then arrives home.

He calls his wife, she answers, rises up, holds out her hand towards her parka, takes it, puts it on, her head shows through the hood, she pulls one sleeve on, then the other. She holds out her hand towards her pants, takes them, pulls one leg on, then the other, pulls it up to her waist. She sits down, holds her hand out to her boots, takes them, puts one on, then the other, she jumps on the floor, ties one string, then the other, takes her mittens, puts one on, then the other, goes towards the porch, bends down, goes through one porch, then the other, goes out, takes the string from her husband's hand, she pulls, goes through one porch, then the other, goes in, closes the door, blocks it on one side, then on the other. She then puts a large stone in front of it. She prepares the food, then puts snow in the cooking pot. Then she heats up the cooking pot, it is warm, she puts pieces of meat into it, twice, thrice. She cooks it, it is cooked, she turns the meat in the pot. Then she takes meat out of the pot, twice, thrice, lets it cool, it is cold. She takes some, chews it, eats the stew, and stops.

He holds his hand out and takes some. His partner tries to come in. He unblocks the door on one side, then the other, then he pushes the big stone, he goes through the door, he comes in, puts his partner out, closes the door, blocks one side, then the other, then he puts the big stone back, then he takes some stew. He eats, and eats, then he puts meat into the cooking pot, twice, thrice, then he cooks it, turns the meat over, then he takes meat, he cools it, it is cool, he puts his hand toward the meat, takes some, chews it, swallows what he has in his mouth, takes more, chews it and leaves off.

After putting meat in the pot three times, it is finished. The skin is cleaned, the fat removed, then it is scraped, then holes are made around the edge, pegs are inserted, it is put to dry. It is dried, they go.

The Faithless Wife
Leah Tataniq and Joanasie Salomonie

The story of the fox-wife is one of the best known in the Arctic. Children from Greenland to Siberia know it, much as Southern children know "Red Riding Hood" or "Hansel and Gretel". Like European fairy-tales, this story has an ending that is violent enough to satisfy even the most bloodthirsty child. This version was recorded on tape by Leah Tataniq at Frobisher Bay in 1966, and transcribed in Inuktitut by Joanasie Salomonie.

A man who was living alone with his wife noticed that she often left the place without his knowing where she went. On his return home from his day-work, he seldom found her at home. This made him suspicious; and one morning he feigned to be going far away, but when he went out in his kayak he only paddled to the nearest point, and went on shore again and hid himself behind some rocks. After a little his wife emerged from the tent in her best attire. He now stole up behind her, and followed her till she reached a lake; there he observed her throw off something into the water, upon which a masculine being appeared, and she undressing, went out to him in the water. At this sight the husband got into a great rage, and set about gathering all kinds of vermin; and one day when he was quite alone with his wife he stuffed them into her, and in this manner killed her. From that day he was all alone, but did not wish to go out in his kayak minding his usual business. One day, on his returning to his lonely tent, he was very much surprised to find his supper cooked, and the smoking meat served up. The next day the same thing happened again; the meat smoking hot was served up on his dish, and his boots were dried and ready to put on; and all this was repeated every day. One day he only paddled a little way off the coast, and then went on shore to hide in a place, whence he could keep a look-out on his tent; and he soon observed a little woman, with her hair dressed up in a very large tuft, come down the hill and enter his tent. He now quickly made for his kayak, paddled home, and went creeping up to his house. Having softly lifted the door-curtain, he noticed a strong unpleasant smell, and saw the little woman busily trimming his lamp. She was really a fox transformed into the shape of a woman, and this accounted for the strong smell. Nevertheless, he took her for his wife. One day he met his cousin out at sea, and told him about his new wife, praising her loveliness, and next asked him to come and see her. "But," added he, "if thou shouldst happen to notice a rank smell about her, be sure not to make any remarks about it." The cousin followed him at once, and having landed together they both entered the tent. But when the visitor observed how nice and pleasant the wife of his cousin was, he grew jealous, and in order to make mischief exclaimed, "Whence comes this nasty smell?" Instantly the little woman rose to her feet: she had now got a tail, wherewith she extinguished the lamp, and like a fox cried, "Ka, ka, ka!" and ran out of the tent. The husband followed her quickly, but when he again caught sight of her she was transformed into a fox, running uphill as fast as possible. He pursued her, and at last she vanished into a cave. It is told that while he stood outside calling for her, she first sent him a beetle, and then a spider, and at last a caterpillar. He then grew quite enraged, heaped some fuel together at the entrance, and burned her alive; and once more he was quite alone, and at last killed himself in a fit of madness.

Leah Tataniq and Joanasie Salomonie   161

How Noisy They Seem
Alootook Ipellie

There is irony in the fact that the civilization which is disrupting the old Inuit culture also provides the technology which is the only means of preserving it—on film. Almost every single person in the Arctic today seems to be a "camera nut". This poem by Ipellie captures some of the feelings that old photographs evoke.

I saw a picture today, in the pages of a book.
It spoke of many memories of when I was still a child:
Snow covered the ground,
And the rocky hills were cold and grey with frost.
The sun was shining from the west,
And the shadows were dark against the whiteness of the
    hardened snow.

My body felt a chill
Looking at two Inuit boys playing with their sleigh,
For the fur of their hoods was frosted under their chins,
From their breathing.
In the distance, I could see at least three dog teams going away,
But I didn't know where they were going,
For it was only a photo.
I thought to myself that they were probably going hunting,
To where they would surely find some seals basking on the ice.
Seeing these things made me feel good inside,
And I was happy that I could still see the hidden beauty of the
    land,
And know the feeling of silence,

Fresh and free.
That's how it used to be,
Before the settlers came and brought their noise.
How noisy they seem...

We Must Have Dreams
John Amagoalik

John Amagoalik is vice president of the Inuit Tapirisat of Canada and a former director of Inuit land claims for the N.W.T. *In this essay he discusses a concern that is shared by Inuit everywhere in Canada: the survival of their culture. The piece first appeared in* Inuit Today *in 1977.*

Will the Inuit disappear from the face of this earth? Will we become extinct? Will our culture, our language and our attachment to nature be remembered only in history books? These questions bring a great sadness to me. To realize that we Inuit are in the same category as the great whales, the bold eagle, the husky and the polar bear brings me great fear. To realize that our people can be classified as an endangered species is very disturbing. Is our culture like a wounded polar bear that has gone out to sea to die alone? What can be done? There does not seem to be one single answer to these questions.

It may be true that the physical part of our culture has been eroded to the point where it can never return to its full potential. But the non-physical part of our culture—our attitude towards life, our respect for nature, our realization that others will follow who deserve the respect and concern of present generations—are deeply entrenched within ourselves. The presence of our ancestors within ourselves is very strong. The will to survive is there. This part of our culture will die a slow death, if it ever dies at all. If we are to survive as a race, we must have the understanding and patience of the dominant cultures of this country. We do not need the pity, the welfare, the paternalism and the colonialism which has been heaped upon us over the years.

We must teach our children their mother tongue. We must teach them what they are and where they came from. We must teach them the values which have guided our society over the thousands of years. We must teach them our philosophies which go back beyond the memory of man. We must keep the embers burning from the fires which used to burn in our villages so that we may gather around them again. It is this spirit we must keep alive so that it may guide us again in a new life in a changed world. Who is responsible for keeping this spirit alive? It is clearly the older people. We must have the leadership which they once provided us. They must realize this responsibility and accept it. If the older people will remember, the young must listen.

In a world which becomes more complicated with each passing year, we must rely on the simple, gentle ways of our people to guide us. In a world so full of greed, we must share. We must remember that, of all the things in this world, nothing belongs to us. Of what we take, we must share.

A lot of people tell me that we must forget the past, and instead, look to the future. To me it would be a mistake to completely ignore the past because the past determines the present and the present determines what will be in the future. Sometimes it is necessary to look to the past to make decisions about the future. When I talk about the future and try to describe what I would like for my children, some people sometimes say to me that I am only dreaming. What is wrong with dreaming? Sometimes dreams come true, if only one is determined enough. What kind of world would we live in if people did not have dreams? If people did not strive for what they believe in? We must have dreams. We must have ideals. We must fight for things we believe in. We must believe in ourselves. But there are also realities we must face. We can only attempt to make the best of any given situation or circumstances. If we are not successful, we must not give up hope. We must tell ourselves that we can only try a little harder the next time.

Over the past few years, in my visits to Inuit communities, I have had many private conversations about what is happening to our people and what the future holds for us. I have become more and more concerned about the angry words which some of our people are starting to use. I cannot really blame them for their feelings. Their feelings towards the white man are easy to understand. It is very easy to blame the white man for the predicament we find ourselves in today. But anger and hate are not the answers. We need the patience and understanding of our white brothers. If we are to expect that from them, we must offer the same in return. The Inuit, by nature, are not violent people. This is one of our virtues which we must not lose.

It disturbs me a great deal to hear about native organizations squabbling with other native organizations. If we are to achieve anything, we must not fight among ourselves. We can agree to disagree, but we must sort out our problems together. We must be of one mind and of one voice. This is not always possible among human beings. But we must not let petty disagreements divide us.

The Inuit were once strong, independent and proud people. That is why we have survived. That strength, that independence, and that pride must surface again. We must prove to Canada that the original citizens of this country will not lie down and play dead. After all, the Inuit have been described by the United Nations as a people who refuse to disappear.

John Amagoalik 165

Acknowledgements

The editor and the publisher wish to extend grateful acknowledgement to the following for use of the material quoted. Apology is made for any errors or omissions. After diligent enquiry, a number of copyright owners have not been located, and the publishers would be grateful for information enabling them to make suitable acknowledgement in future editions.

Taivitialuk Alaasuaq for "The Half-Fish" from *Eskimo Stories/Unikkaatuat*, edited by Nungak and Arima, National Museum of Man, National Museums of Canada, Ottawa.

John Amagoalik for "We Must Have Dreams" from *Inuit Today*, Vol. VI, No. 4, May 1977.

Martha Angugaatiaq for "First Aid Among the Eskimos" from *Inummarit*, Vol. II, No. 1.

Jeanne Arnainuk for "Cup and Ball Game: Ajagarniq" from *Inummarit*, Vol. I, No. 4.

Canadian Arctic Producers for "I Make My Living by Carving" by Marius Kayotak from *We Don't Live in Snow Houses Now*, edited by Susan Cowan.

Department of Indian & Northern Affairs for "Akeeko Is Writing" by Akeeko from *Northern Welfare 62; A Symposium on Northern Social Work*; for "Remembering Old Times" by Simon Arnaviapik from *Inuktitut*, Fall 1974; for "The Story of John Ayaruaq" by John Ayaruaq from *North/Nord*, Vol. XVI, No. 2, March 1969; for "A Spring Seal Hunt" by Eepilk from *North/Nord*, Vol. XVI, No. 4, July 1969; for "In the Spring When the Sun Never Sets" by Lucy Evaloardjuak from *Inuktitut*, Summer 1972; for "The Little Arctic Tern, the Big Polar Bear" by Leah Idlout from *North/Nord*, Vol. VI, No. 4, September 1959; for "Marble Island" by Leonie Kappi from *North/Nord*, Vol. XVIII, No. 6, November 1971; for "Song of Markoosie" by Markoosie from *Inuktitut*, Summer 1967; for "The

Whale and the Char" (Anonymous) from *Inuktitut*, Summer 1972; for "Morning Mood" by Mary Panegoosho from *Northern Welfare 62; A Symposium on Northern Social Work*; for "Where Are the Stories of My People?" by Mary Panegoosho from *North/Nord*, Vol. IX, No. 5, September 1962; for "The Many Lives of Anakajuttuq" by Joe Panipakuttuk from *North/Nord*, Vol. XVI, No. 5, September 1969; for "Akulak the Shaman" by Mrs. Louis Tapatai from *Inuktitut*, Winter 1972; for "The Faithless Wife" by Leah Tataniq and Joanasie Salomonie from *Inuktitut*, Summer 1967.

Minnie Aodla Freeman for *Survival in the South*.

Griffin House for "So You Want to Kill an Eskimo" by Anthony Apakark Thrasher from *Skid Row Eskimo*.

Leah Idlout for "Wonderful Life" from *Inuit Today*, Vol. IV, No. 10, November 1975.

Inuit Tapirisat of Canada for "Ululigarqnaarq" (Anonymous) from *Inuit Monthly*, Vol. III, No. 9.

Laimiki Innuaraq for "A Sad Case" from *Midnight Sun Newsletter*, December 1972.

Alootook Ipellie for "How Noisy They Seem" from *Inuit Today*, Vol. V, No. 1, January 1976; for "Nipikti the Old Man Carver" from *Inukshuk*, Vol. III, No. 50, February 1976; for "N.W.T. Separates from Canada" from *Inuit Today*, Vol. VI, No. 6, July 1977; for "One of Those Wonderful Nights" from *Inuit Monthly*, Vol. III, No. 4, April 1974.

Ivaluardjuk for "A Song" from *Midnight Sun Newsletter*, November 1969.

Mark Kalluak for "Mahaha the Tickler" by Marcel Akadlaka from *How Kabloonat Became and Other Legends*, edited by Mark Kalluak, Program Development Division, Dept. of Education, Govt. of the N.W.T.; for "Story of Inukshuk" from *Keewatin Echo*, No. 59, May 1973.

Kiakshuk for "The Giant Bear" from *Songs and Stories of the Netsilik Eskimos*, edited by Edward Field, Educational Development Centre, Massachusetts.

Ohokto and L.A. Learmonth for "Ross Meets the Netchiliks" from *The Beaver*, Vol. 279, September 1948.

Charlie Patsauq for "The Custom" from *Inukshuk*, Vol. II, No. 21, June 1974.

Peter Pitseolak and Dorothy Eber for "The First Religious Time" from *People from Our Side*, translated by Anne Hanson, Hurtig Publishers, Edmonton.

PMA Books, Toronto for "Kaivitjvik—Polar Night Festivals" by Nuligak from *I, Nuligak*, edited by Maurice Metayer.

Francois Tamnaruluk for "Song for the Mitcheners" from *Midnight Sun Newsletter*, November 1969.

Marion Tuu'luq and Susan Tagoona for "A Story of Starvation" from *Inuit Today*, Vol. VI, No. 9, November 1977.

Alexis Utatnaq for "Blood-thirsty Enemies" from *Keewatin Echo*, No. 71, June 1974.

John Weetaltuk for "Land" from *Inukshuk*, Vol. III, No. 46, January 1976.

Recommended Books

In addition to the books and publications listed in the Acknowledgements, readers may also be interested in the following books by Inuit authors:

Arnaktauyok, Germaine, illustrator. *Stories from Pangnirtung*. Edmonton: Hurtig, 1976.

Freeman, Minnie Aodla. *Life Among the Qallunaat*. Edmonton: Hurtig, 1978.

French, Alice. *My Name is Masak*. Winnipeg: Peguis, 1977.

Green, Paul, aided by Abbe Abbot. *I Am Eskimo, Aknik My Name*. Illustrated by George Ahgupuk. Juneau, Alaska: Alaska Northwest Publishing Co., 1959.

Hoffman, Charles. *Drum Dance: Legends, Ceremonies, Dances and Songs of the Eskimos*. Canada: Gage, 1974.

Kappi, Leonie, ed. *Inuit Legends*. Illustrated by Germaine Arnaktauyok. Yellowknife: Dept. of Education, Govt. of the N.W.T., 1977.

Lowenstein, Tom. *Eskimo Poems from Canada and Greenland*. From material originally collected by Knud Rasmussen. London: Anchor Press, 1973.

Markoosie. *Harpoon of the Hunter*. Illustrated by Germaine Arnaktauyok. Montreal: McGill-Queens University Press, 1970.

Metayer, Maurice. *Tales from the Igloo*. Illustrated by Agnes Nanogak. Edmonton: Hurtig, 1972.

Padlayat, Josepi, ed. *The Northerners*. Toronto: Northern Quebec Inuit Association, 1974.

Pitseolak. *Pitseolak: Pictures Out of My Life*. Edited by Dorothy Eber. Montreal: Oxford University Press, 1971.

Pitseolak, Peter. *Peter Pitseolak's Escape from Death*. Edited by Dorothy Eber. Toronto: McClelland and Stewart, 1977.

Related Reading

Briggs, Jean L. *Never in Anger: Portrait of an Eskimo Family.* Cambridge, Mass.: Harvard University Press, 1970.

Bruemmer, Fred. *Seasons of the Eskimo: A Vanishing Way of Life.* Toronto/Montreal: McClelland and Stewart, 1971.

Crowe, Keith J. *A History of the Original Peoples of Northern Canada.* Montreal: McGill-Queens University Press, 1974.

Erngaard, Erik. *Greenland Then and Now.* Copenhagen: Lademann, 1972.

Gedalof, Robin. *An Annotated Bibliography of Canadian Inuit Literature.* Ottawa: Dept. of Indian and Northern Affairs, 1979.

Goudie, Elizabeth. *Woman of Labrador.* Edited by David Zimmerly. Toronto: PMA Books, 1973.

Lyall, Ernie. *An Arctic Man: Sixty-five Years in Canada's North.* Edmonton: Hurtig, 1979.

Mallon, S.T. *Inuktitut Phase One* and *Inuktitut Phase Two.* Yellowknife: Dept. of Education, Govt. of the N.W.T., 1976.

Marsh, Winifred Petchey. *People of the Willow: The Padlimiut Tribe of the Caribou Eskimo.* Toronto: Oxford University Press, 1976.

Mowat, William and Christine, eds. *Native Peoples in Canadian Literature.* Toronto: Macmillan, 1975.

Moyles, R.G. *British Law and Arctic Men.* Saskatoon: Western Producer Prairie Books, 1979.

Sissons, Jack. *Judge of the Far North.* Toronto: McClelland and Stewart, 1973.

Designer/David Shaw
Typesetter/Attic Typesetting
Manufacturer/John Deyell Company